C000276992

The
Connell Guide
to
Shakespeare's

———

The Tempest

———

by
Graham Bradshaw

Contents

What is distinctive about
Shakespeare's use of language in
The Tempest?

How seriously should we take
Prospero when he argues that life
itself is an illusion?

So what view of the world does
Shakespeare leave us with at the
end of *The Tempest*?

NOTES

Introduction

In the 400 years since *The Tempest* was first
staged, millions of words have been written about
it. Critics, directors and actors have interpreted
it in widely different ways and developed theories
ranging from the more-or-less plausible to
the eccentric and the completely outlandish.

It is undoubtedly one of Shakespeare's greatest
plays, and as well as its bewitching music, its
hallucinatory quality and its enchanted island
setting, it contains some of Shakespeare's most
beautiful poetry and most famous lines. From
Caliban's "The isle is full of noises" to Prospero's
"We are such stuff/As dreams are made on",
The Tempest haunts our collective imagination.

But what is it actually about? Is it about British
colonialism, as so many modern critics, especially
modern American critics, firmly maintain? Is it a
Christian play? Or is it, as Sir Peter Hall believes,
the "most blasphemous play Shakespeare wrote",
about a "man on an island who's allowed to play
God and who doesn't just dabble in witchcraft
but actually performs it"?

Is it an anti-feminist play, as some feminist
critics believe? Or does it, on the contrary – in
common with Shakespeare's late plays – present
a softer, more feminised view of the world than
his earlier works? And what does *The Tempest*, the
last play Shakespeare wrote on his own, tell us

about his view of art, and of the human condition?

This short guide sets out to answer these and other questions. Its aim is to illuminate the text, as clearly and concisely as possible, and to show what an extraordinary work of art *The Tempest* is. It draws on and discusses the most interesting and arresting criticisms of the play, explains the issues which have perplexed and divided scholars through the ages, and, most importantly, offers a bold, incisive and authoritative view of its own.

THE CHARACTERS

PROSPERO, *the rightful Duke of Milan*

MIRANDA, *a daughter to Prospero*

ANTONIO, *his brother, the usurping Duke of Milan*

ALONSO, *King of Naples*

SEBASTIAN, *his brother*

FERDINAND, *Alonso's son*

GONZALO, *an honest old Councillor of Naples*

ADRIAN and FRANCISCO, *Lords*

ARIEL, *an airy spirit*

CALIBAN, *a savage and deformed slave of Prospero's*

TRINCULO, *a jester*

STEPHANO, *a drunken butler*

MASTER *of a ship*

BOATSWAIN

MARINERS

Spirits appearing as Iris, Ceres, Juno, nymphs and reapers

A summary of the plot

Act One

In a fiercely realistic first scene, a terrible
tempest batters a ship returning from Tunis to
Naples. Aboard are Alonso, King of Naples, his
brother, Sebastian, and son Ferdinand, Antonio,
Duke of Milan, and Gonzalo, an old and trusted
councillor. Shipwrecked, they are cast ashore
on a strange and apparently deserted island,
unaware that the tempest has been caused
by the magic of Prospero, the former Duke of
Milan, who now lives on the island with his
daughter, Miranda.

Questioned by Miranda, Prospero relates
how they arrived on the island twelve years
earlier: as Duke of Milan, he had handed some
duties to his brother Antonio who, gaining a
taste for power, usurped Prospero with the aid
of Alonso. Cast adrift in a small boat, Prospero
and the young Miranda eventually landed on
the island, where they found the half-human,
half-savage Caliban and the spirit Ariel. Prospero
made Ariel his servant and Caliban his slave.
Now, told by Ariel that he at last has his enemies
where he wants them, Prospero the magician
moves to the next stage of his plan. He lures
Ferdinand into his presence and encourages
him and Miranda to fall in love, while pretending
to disapprove.

Act Two

Alonso and his companions are searching for
Ferdinand. Ariel, who remains invisible, sends
everyone to sleep except Antonio, the usurping
Duke of Milan, and Sebastian, Alonso's brother.
The two men plot to murder Alonso and the
courtier Gonzalo while they lie asleep, but Ariel
prevents this by waking everyone up just in time.
On another part of the island, Trinculo, the jester,
comes across Caliban, to their mutual surprise;
when the drunken butler, Stephano, arrives,
Caliban thinks he must be a god and offers to serve
him in the hope of escaping Prospero's control.

Act Three

Prospero has enslaved Ferdinand and made him
carry logs, but Ferdinand does so willingly in order
to serve his beloved Miranda. Watched secretly by
a delighted Prospero, the two pledge to marry each
other. Caliban tells Trinculo and Stephano that he
is Prospero's slave; he proposes that they murder
the magician, and that Stephano marry Miranda
and rule in Prospero's stead. Alonso and his party,
meanwhile, have given up hope of finding Ferdinand
when, to the sound of strange music, spirits
materialise in front of them and produce a banquet.
Before they can eat, however, Ariel appears, and
makes the banquet vanish. Ariel then taunts Alonso,
Antonio and Sebastian for their part in trying
to kill "good Prosper" and his "innocent daughter".

Act Four

Prospero admits that the tasks he set Ferdinand were to test his love for Miranda, and he now blesses their marriage with a masque performed by spirits. Then he suddenly remembers Caliban's plot against his life, angrily halts the performance and calls Ariel to him. He despatches Ariel to fetch the hapless Caliban and his accomplices. They are brought to Prospero's cell, where they are then chased by spirits disguised as hunting dogs. Prospero rejoices that all of his enemies are finally at his mercy, promising Ariel he will soon be free.

Act Five

Ariel reports that Alonso and the other Neapolitans are broken men, and Prospero tells Ariel to fetch them. Alone, he promises to give up his magic powers. When the chastened group arrive, they are amazed to find Prospero, who fiercely reprimands the "three men of sin" who conspired to exile him. Prospero then reveals Ferdinand and Miranda, playing chess, to Alonso's great joy. Prospero forgives his enemies, releases Ariel, acknowledges Caliban as "my own" and announces that they will all return to Naples where he will resume his role as Duke.

What is *The Tempest* about?

The Tempest has often been described as Shakespeare's most elusive play. The director Peter Brook calls it "an enigma", while the critic Anne Barton describes it as "an extraordinarily obliging work of art that will lend itself to almost any interpretation". Certainly, it has been read and staged in widely different ways over the years.

Many critics have seen it as a "serene" play about Christian forgiveness, with Prospero as a kind of Christ-figure who – like Duke Vincentio in the final scene of *Measure for Measure* – refuses to punish his enemies. There are difficulties with this Christian reading. Christianity does not have a monopoly on mercy and forgiveness, and Prospero does not decide to be merciful until the final scene. It never occurred to earlier, great and profoundly Christian critics like Dr Johnson or Coleridge that they should be regarding Prospero – or Duke Vincentio – as Christ-figures. Finally, there is no reference to Christianity in the play.

There have been many other allegorical readings, which explain the play as an account of survival after death, or even as an allegory of the history of the Church. The more familiar idea that Prospero is Shakespeare and that *The Tempest* represents Shakespeare's farewell to his art is also allegorical, as well as Romantic, and was first propounded by Thomas Campbell in 1838; it was most elaborately developed by Montégut in his argument that the play presents an "account, feature by feature, of the English theatre and transformation to which Shakespeare subjected it". Rather surprisingly, Montégut's thesis was further elaborated in 1991 by the distinguished critic René Girard. There were many passionate readers of allegory in Shakespeare's lifetime, but we have no record that any of his contemporaries thought any of Shakespeare's plays were allegorical. A. D. Nuttall, whose study, *Two Concepts of Allegory*, thoroughly explores the question of whether *The Tempest* is allegorical, concludes that it is not. As the American scholar Professor Harold Bloom succinctly puts it: "Allegory was not a Shakespearean mode."

More recently, the teaching of Shakespeare in university English departments has been powerfully influenced by so-called American "New Historicist" and British "cultural materialist" critics.* These critics have been most concerned with the political significance of *The Tempest* as a colonialist text, in which Prospero is the grasping colonial invader and Caliban the innocent native victim. They have also revived the 19th-century idea that *The*

* New Historicism is a school of literary theory developed in the 1980s, primarily through the work of the critic Stephen Greenblatt: it aims to understand works through their historical context, and cultural and intellectual history through literature. Cultural materialism, a similar movement, traces its origins to the British critic Raymond Williams. The term was coined by him to describe a theoretical blending of Leftist culturalism and Marxist analysis.

Tempest is a play about the New World.

This way of reading *The Tempest* is now very influential, and is perhaps still dominant. These critics frequently and sometimes effectively draw on the extraordinarily rich and suggestive range of "native" African, West Indian, and Latin American responses to *The Tempest*. But inevitably they are preoccupied with the relationship between Prospero and Caliban. They barely discuss Ariel, and, in their obsession with the political "message", often treat Shakespeare's poetic drama as though it were – or might as well have been – written in prose.

In fact, as the play's second scene shows, the relationship between Prospero and Caliban is just one of a whole web of different familial, master-servant and political relationships in the play. At the centre of the web, of course, is Prospero. We first see him with his daughter Miranda, who is deeply worried about whether – to put it simply – her magician-father is a good man. We then see Prospero with the spirit Ariel, who is forced to carry out his commands, then with the enslaved Caliban, and finally with Prince Ferdinand. We see him becoming enraged with all of them, even with Miranda, when she attempts to defend Ferdinand.

All of these different relationships are power relationships – as Prospero's rages confirm. So, if we are attending to this whole web or nexus of relationships when we ask what this play is about, it makes good sense to suppose that it is about power – or, as Harold Bloom suggests, authority.

Among those who argue this case compellingly is the critic Russ McDonald. One of *The Tempest*'s primary concerns, he says, is the "problem of power". He means political power, of course, the power wielded by Prospero and the assorted villains who land on his island. But he means more than that, as we will see later, extending his argument to include the power of art itself, and of the playwright to manipulate us – his audience. McDonald shows how the play's very distinctive poetry reinforces this theme, and maintains that to listen to the language of *The Tempest* "is to become deeply sceptical about the operation of all kinds of power – poetic, political, and critical too".

What does the play tell us about power?

In its subtle, sometimes bitter and not at all serene way, the play elaborates Lord Acton's famous maxim that "All power corrupts, and absolute power corrupts absolutely." Some recent critics see Shakespeare as a kind of court lackey, loyally or desperately anxious to please the monarch. Yet this play's presentation of rulers like Antonio, Alonso and indeed Prospero himself suggests that many or most rulers are either idle, or incompetent

Opposite: Alastair Sim as Prospero in an Old Vic production, London, 1962

or vicious, if not all three.

The viciousness of two of the three rulers in the play, Alonso and Antonio, is not in doubt. But it is clear from Prospero's own account of his years as Duke of Milan that he, too, was a bad ruler. Like Marlowe's Doctor Faustus, he was obsessed with learning. He took his position and privileges for granted while wholly neglecting the duties of office – like King Lear, and like Duke Vincentio. For years, he delegated such responsibilities to his younger brother, Antonio, while he pursued his studies in the "liberal arts" and magic. Of course Antonio eventually decided he wanted to have the position and all the privileges and rewards of power as well. Indeed, once – and only once, but it is a telling moment in the play's second scene – Prospero acknowledges that he and his own misrule had "awaked" his brother's "evil nature".

The first scene, which otherwise provides no clues about where the play is going, includes another such telling, resonant moment when the ship is heading for the rocks of the nearby island where Prospero was shipwrecked 12 years earlier, and Sycorax 12 years before that. The Boatswain is desperately fighting, and fast losing, a battle for survival. He has no time to touch the forelock or think, like Macduff in the first – though not the second – half of *Macbeth*, that a king is "the Lord's anointed". He rudely orders his royal passengers back to their cabins and points at the waves: "What care these roarers for the name of king?" When set against this annihilating natural force, man's artificial ranks and divisions count for nothing.

They cannot be "read off", as the philosopher Ludwig Wittgenstein memorably remarked about human values in general: he meant that they are not solid – not part of the non-human world's fabric or furniture. Rather, they are human constructs, or "foundational fictions". In our human world we quite rightly do not want to surrender all such beliefs, or illusions, for that would be to surrender our humanity – and "human" is a key word in *The Tempest* , because the play is so preoccupied with what it means to be human or (since the words were interchangeable at this time) humane. So, for Prospero, the ceremonies and "holy rites" of marriage are what distinguishes human mating from the matings of other animals, and he is fiercely opposed to pre-marital sex.

Shakespeare's sceptical exploration of power has a long history. In his early history plays – the three parts of *Henry VI* and *Richard III* – young Shakespeare had tried, in a rather sweatily loyal way, to endorse or at least not question the absolute and increasingly absolutist Tudor and Stuart dogma that kings rule by divine right, and that even a "tyrant" may be God's judgement on a sinful people. But Shakespeare abandoned this effort in his next historical play, *King John*, which is still seldom discussed or given the weight it deserves. After that,

the plays question whatever can be questioned –
but not in the playwright's own voice. Knowing
what Shakespeare himself believed is far more
difficult than knowing what later dramatists
like Brecht and Shaw, or Chekhov, Ibsen, and
Beckett believed.

In *King John*, as the "Bastard" sees and says,
power is *de facto*, something that the king has
seized and then – like Henry IV and Henry V in
Shakespeare's second historical tetralogy – strives
to present as God's will. This is not to say, like the
American critic Stephen Greenblatt, that Henry IV
and Henry V are "hypocrites". They care about
their country, in a way that the various rebels never
do. But they always believe that England's interests
somehow and miraculously coincide with those of
the Lancastrian family or dynasty.

These plays never affirm or deny that belief
or foundational fiction. More generally, what
Shakespeare's plays do instead is show how
differently different characters think and feel
about their own situations, and about issues like
love, or honour, or the divine right of kings. The
plays then become complex designs, in which
there is a highly organised interplay of different
voices and views, but no sure way of telling which
character speaks with Her or His Master's voice.
For Macduff, in the first part of *Macbeth*, King
Duncan is "the Lord's anointed". For Lady
Macbeth, Duncan is "the old man" in her way.

If *The Tempest* is so sceptical about power, why did James I like it?

Far more obviously than *King John*, *Macbeth* is another landmark that looks forward to *The Tempest* in its thinking about kings and tyrants and what Russ McDonald calls the problem of power. Oddly, but perhaps not so oddly, surviving records suggest there were only a few performances of *Macbeth* in Shakespeare's lifetime. No record suggests that his contemporaries regarded *Macbeth* as one of his best works. Nor is there any record of a royal performance, although the myth that there was one is still repeated by critics like Stephen Orgel. Nor is there any evidence that Shakespeare wrote the "Scottish play" to please the new Scottish monarch.

What we *can* be sure of is that, if King James ever saw *Macbeth* and managed to stay awake and sober, he would have hated it. He would have approved of the way the early, fervently loyal Macduff speaks about kings, and abandons his own family to serve his beloved country and the man he regards as its rightful king. But this choice for king and country narrows further, so that the tragedy of Macbeth includes the smaller but agonising tragedy of Macduff, who is finally forced to choose *between* his king and his country. After prevaricating for a while, like Banquo, the agonised

Macduff passes the test by choosing to be loyal to his country. He declares that if Macbeth is what he says he is, he is not only unfit to govern but unfit to live. And Macbeth must be killed, not as a usurper who murdered Duncan – Macduff doesn't know that – but because he is a *tyrant*. This is a point of no return. After this the word tyrant echoes throughout the rest of the play.

All across Europe at this time, philosophers and scholars were engaged in a long, often intensely heated and dangerous debate about whether it could ever be right for a subject to kill a king who

---

THE WHEREABOUTS OF SHAKESPEARE'S ISLAND

The first person to be shipwrecked on the island was Sycorax, when she was banished from North Africa as a witch. Prospero and Miranda followed, after being ejected from Milan and set adrift in a boat without sails and oars.

Twelve years later Alonso and the others arrived, after being shipwrecked on their way back from Tunis to Naples.

In 1898, Sidney Lee was the first to argue – and go on arguing for a quarter of a century, during which time he was knighted, as well as benighted – that the island is Bermuda and that Caliban is an "aboriginal American" or "tractable type of Indian": "He is a creature stumbling over the first stepping-stones which lead from savagery to civilization." American scholars quickly entered this congenial field, and in 1902 the Bostonian

was a tyrant. Nothing horrified James I more than the idea that this could ever be right. Yet few spectators and readers have ever felt that it was unbelievably wicked for Macduff to kill the tyrant Macbeth – which was a Shakespearean innovation, and a departure from his historical sources. Moreover, few readers or spectators have ever doubted Macduff's goodness – just as they have never doubted Cordelia's in *King Lear*, or Miranda's in *The Tempest*. Although Shakespeare generally refuses to ventriloquise through his characters, some things come through. He is not,

---

Edward Everett Hale explained that the island's topography showed it was not Bermuda but Cuttyhunk Island, off the coast of Cape Cod.

It defies belief that three batches of shipwreck victims all wound up in Cuttyhunk or some Bermuda Triangle. Since they were obviously shipwrecked on an island somewhere in the Mediterranean, another band of literal-minded literary detectives in the late 19th and early 20th centuries speculated about which Mediterranean island this "must" have been. Some scholarly Sherlocks deduced that it was Corfu or even Lampedusa, but in geographical and topographical terms the leading contender was Pantalaria, which is between Tunis and Italy and is also near the North African port of Calibia, which was on Elizabethan and Jacobean maps of the Mediterranean. Caliban, with his far from splendid physique, was no North American Indian, although, since his mother was North African, he might conceivably have been presented as black – Shakespeare's fourth Moor. ◆

like the artist and aesthete James Joyce's Stephen Dedalus describes in *A Portrait of the Artist as a Young Man*, sitting above everything he creates, paring his nails. He clearly believes tyrants do not deserve to rule.

All of this raises an important question. If Russ McDonald is right to say that *The Tempest* takes a very bleak view of what "power" does to those who pursue or possess it, why did King James *like* the play? Not only was it successfully performed in the Banqueting House at Whitehall in 1611; it was revived and performed again at the Banqueting House in 1613 as part of the celebrations for the wedding of James's daughter, Elizabeth. Yet while James I would have objected strongly to *Macbeth*, he apparently was *not* upset by *The Tempest's* presentation of bad rulers and by the way the play deals with the pursuit and possession of power. Why not?

The answer is that *The Tempest* is a more subtle exploration of power than *Macbeth*: it is a comedy, after all, and the tone is lighter; and the conspiracies which take place in the play are all safely contained. Moreover, Shakespeare covered himself well: Caliban calls Prospero a tyrant, but King James, like many early critics, would probably have taken the view that Prospero's enslavement of Caliban, while harsh, was unavoidable because of Caliban's attempt to rape Miranda.

Opposite: King James I (1566-1625)

Shakespeare's critique of power, however, is much more all-encompassing than James I seems to have realised and this critique undoubtedly extends to Prospero's behaviour on the island. Indeed Shakespeare's view of power seems to have been a good deal more cynical than his monarch would have appreciated. To understand this it is worth looking first at the way Shakespeare structures the play, and then at Prospero's role within it.

How are the themes of the play reflected in its structure?

The plots which animate *The Tempest* are all about seizing power. Prospero is on the island because his brother Antonio forced him out of Milan and nearly killed him. No sooner has the ship hit the rocks in the first scene, and its passengers come ashore, than Antonio is persuading Sebastian that he too should seize power by killing King Alonso. This new plot clearly echoes the original sin of Antonio's treacherous and murderous plot against his brother. It is then echoed again in the next scene, when Caliban persuades Stephano and Trinculo to murder Prospero.

The constant echoes and parallels help account for the ways in which, as A.D. Nuttall and other critics have so often suggested, *The Tempest* seems dream-like. The constant variations have the unstoppability of dreams, and seem like endless refractions of old injuries and obsessions. But, far from being unreal, these dreams recall Karl Marx's warning that if we cannot learn from history we are doomed to repeat it. The dreams echo the blood-drip of history.

The parallels are often subtle. In a strange, even weird way, the scene in which Caliban plots a rebellion that will allow him to serve a new master, Stephano, is then echoed in Act Three's betrothal scene. Each of these scenes begins with a soliloquy in which a victim of Prospero's rage to control everything and everyone – first Caliban, then Ferdinand – enters lugging logs, and complaining about Prospero. We see how Caliban "adores" and longs to "serve" the first man he has ever seen, apart from Prospero – Stephano, the new "master" who excites him with liquor. We then see how Miranda "adores" and longs to "serve" Ferdinand, who is, as she says, only the third man she has ever seen – after her father and the allegedly non-human Caliban. Caliban plots his rebellion, and Miranda, at the same time, begins to rebel against her father.

The echoes keep multiplying. Prospero's long narrative in the second scene allows – just once, but that is enough – that his own bad government had *"awaked"* his brother's "evil nature". Prospero was then a victim, who trusted and loved his brother.

But in Act Two, when he is an all-powerful agent whose magic no other character can resist, he instructs Ariel to send Alonso, Gonzalo and the others to *sleep*, so that Antonio and Sebastian can plot their latest evil. Is Prospero wanting to confirm what Antonio's real nature is really like, by leading him into temptation?

In this last respect, the play looks forward to Milton's *Paradise Lost* where Milton's all-knowing, all foreseeing God first builds Hell in advance, knowing that Satan's rebellion will occur, and fail – and then allows Satan to enter Eden, knowing in advance that Adam and Eve will then fall. Of course, Milton's God gave Adam and Eve "free will" when he created them, so that they are in that technical-theological sense free not to fall, although God very well knows that they will fall. Since language shows where we are, and sometimes measures the punishing distance between where we are and wherever we meant to be, consider what the purposive "that" means – if not "in order that", or "so that" – in the sentence where Milton explains that God "left" Satan

> *to his dark designs,*
> *That with reiterated crimes he might*
> *Heap on himself damnation...*

Prospero instructs Ariel to send Alonso back to sleep, so that Antonio can "reiterate" his own earlier crime.

The Tempest is like some existential dance in a hall of mirrors.* The impression it gives is of life repeating itself: people act in similar ways; the errors of the past are repeated. (Prospero's account of his past to his daughter, itself a repetition, as we are made aware, of similar accounts, dwells constantly on the mistakes of the past.) Rulers and would-be rulers act with the same self-interested ruthlessness as their forebears; the old world has little to teach the new. History doesn't advance; if anything it is regressive rather than progressive – one idea running through the play is the inability to be rid of evil. What has happened before will happen again, or – as Antonio puts it (recalling *Macbeth*), "what's past is prologue". And good genes are no defence against overweening ambition. "Good wombs have borne bad sons," says Miranda. "So it goes," as the narrator/protagonist of Kurt Vonnegut's *Slaughterhouse Five* keeps saying.

* Consider another very curious example of these constantly multiplying echoes, repetitions and "reiterations". When Ferdinand is speaking of all those who were (as he thinks) lost in *The Tempest* he refers to Antonio's "brave son". This allows us a rare peep into Shakespeare's workshop. Evidently Shakespeare had once planned that Antonio should have a son and presumably a wife – and then abandoned that idea while leaving behind this curious trace or textual footprint. Antonio is a monster, but even he would remember if he had lost a son, like King Alonso. At some stage the rhyming of Alonso's and Antonio's sons was probably intended to set up similar contrasts and parallels – if, for example, they were rivals for Miranda's love. As it is, both sons are thought to have been "lost", but one remains forever missing.

Are we meant to sympathise with Prospero?

Some critics certainly have sympathised with him, like the British scholar Geoffrey Bullough, who in 1975 described Prospero as a "good, authoritarian Governor" who knows how to deal with "layabouts", or like all those critics (from Thomas Campbell in 1838 to René Girard in 1991) who have seen Prospero as Shakespeare's self-portrait in a final farewell to his art. The bardolatrous Campbell seems to have been the first to propose that *The Tempest* "has a sort of sacredness as the last work of the mighty workman", and that "Shakespeare, as if conscious that it would be his last, and as if inspired to typify himself, has made its hero a natural, a dignified, and benevolent magician." Today, we are very unlikely to sympathise with Prospero – although our own attitudes to him will also depend, in part, on what we bring to the show.

So Harold Bloom is certainly exaggerating when he declares that "No audience has ever liked Prospero". But he is also pointing to a real difficulty. Prospero has been treated badly, and has responded badly. Like King Lear, he is tortured by what has been done to him, not by what he has done or failed to do for others.

When we first see him and hear him reassuring

his distraught daughter that "There's no harm done", and that he has

> *done nothing but in care of thee,*
> *Of thee, my dear one, thee, my daughter, [1.2]*

his words seem to come from the heart. We are likely to feel some kind of provisional sympathy, although we are and will for a long time remain in the dark about why Prospero has caused the terrible tempest.

But we soon learn that his plan to marry his daughter to King Alonso's son, Ferdinand, is entangled with self-interest, and is part of a larger, strategically political plan to regain his own position as ruler of Milan, and ally the state of Milan with that of Naples.

There is yet another parallel here. Miranda's fate, as the critic Ann Thompson has argued, can be seen as exactly similar to that of Claribel, the daughter of King Alonso, who has been summarily and without any say in the matter married off to the King of Tunis.* Miranda, like Claribel, is at the mercy of her father's wishes and ambitions. So there is a question about Prospero's motives, and whether, as he tells Miranda, "I have done nothing but in care of thee."

Nor will it do to argue that *The Tempest* was

---

*It is on the voyage back from the marriage ceremony in Tunis that the shipwreck at the start of *The Tempest* occurs.

written at a time when a daughter was expected to accept whatever husband her father chose for her, especially when her father was royal and needed to make a dynastic alliance – like King James, when he married his daughter Elizabeth to the Protestant Prince Frederick of Bohemia in 1613. That expectation was still alive, especially in the older generation. But it was already the subject of debate years earlier, when Shakespeare composed *Romeo and Juliet*. Although that play elicits a small measure of sympathy for Juliet's well-meaning but obtuse and distant, unloving father, the play's and our sympathies are far more obviously aligned with Juliet – who is 14, like Miranda. Fortunately, Miranda immediately falls in love with Ferdinand. But it is uncertain whether she would still be forced to marry even if she didn't like the man her father had chosen – like Juliet, and like Claribel, Alonso's daughter.

So it is no surprise to find the formidable Ann Thompson aligning herself with all those critics who dislike Prospero – and who assume, more questionably, that if there is something wrong with Prospero, there is something wrong with this play. Thompson asks, with great asperity: "What kind of pleasure can a woman and a feminist take in this text beyond the rather grim one of mapping its various forms of exploitation?"

And then – right up to this play's very last scene

Opposite: Jasper Britton as Caliban in a production at The Globe, 2000

– we have to reckon with Prospero's constant rages and cruelty. In the long second scene, which provides the play's exposition, we can understand and sympathise with his inner tempest of anger when he is telling Miranda how they were both victims of atrocious wrongs. But in the rest of the scene we see him flying into one rage after another, with Ariel, and then with Caliban, and then with Ferdinand. His rage with Ferdinand is calculated, since he does not want the wooing to be too quick. But that just reminds us how intent Prospero is on controlling everything and everybody else.

When the second scene begins it is clear that even the loving, still obedient Miranda fears her father and thinks him capable of being pitiless. Much later – in the play's penultimate scene (unusually, the last two acts of *The Tempest* only have one scene apiece) – Prospero forgets about Caliban's conspiracy. The frightened Ariel, who knows his master even better than Miranda knows her father, explains:

I thought to have told thee of it, but I fear'd
Lest I might anger thee. [4.1]

Prospero's constant rages are one reason why many contemporary critics, notably Stephen Orgel and Margreta da Grazia, have rejected Frank Kermode's distinction between Prospero's "holy" magic and Sycorax's "devilish" magic. As Orgel protests, there is "nothing whatever in the play implying that Sycorax's ministers are devils, or that the spirits she controls are any lower, or indeed any other, than those 'weak masters' at Prospero's command". Ariel "is the unwilling servant of both", and "as the play progresses, the similarities between the two sorcerors grow increasingly marked". This echoes Margreta da Grazia's argument that "Not only are [Prospero's and Sycorax's] histories similar and their powers interchangeable, but both sorceress and magician are driven by the same passion – anger." (See p. 32)

Finally, audiences must reckon with Prospero's cruelty. Although Prospero threatens Ariel and Ferdinand with the most dreadul tortures, he never does torture Ariel, who is in any case his chief torturer, and the only pain and humiliation he inflicts on Ferdinand is that of having to carry "thousands" of logs from one place to another. But he does torture Caliban, regularly, and the tortures he devises to inflict on him are so ingeniously sadistic that they show how, for Prospero, torturing those who don't obey his commands is a pleasure as well as a duty.

Why has Prospero been so vilified in recent years?

Critics like Derek Traversi went on defending such cruelty long after the British Empire had fallen apart, along with many of the justifications for it. Seeing the play through Prospero's eyes, he explained that "Caliban is bound by his nature to service". As that chilling phrase might remind us, for two thousand years philosophers from Aristotle to David Hume had defended slavery by arguing that some people or, worse, peoples, are

PROSPERO'S MAGIC

The Renaissance saw the rise of "philosopher-scientist-magicians" (in a pre-scientific age these categories merged together) – men seeking the Philosopher's Stone, alchemists, conjurers and sorcerers, all of whom laid claims to esoteric knowledge. There was also, inevitably, a rise in conmen seeking to exploit contemporary gullibility: Ben Jonson's brilliant and funny play, *The Alchemist*, shows two conmen in action, spouting semi-learned gobbledygook to fleece their greedy and foolish customers.

People were passionately concerned with the difference between black or devilish magic and good "natural" magic, and academics have often argued over the forms of magic practised in *The Tempest*. In 1954, Frank Kermode contrasted the bad "natural magic" in the play with Prospero's supposedly

"natural" slaves. In a famous, blisteringly funny but lethal 1964 essay, "Hunt the Symbol", William Empson exposed and exploded the imperialist assumptions that made critics like Traversi so unwilling to consider Caliban's point of view. Traversi, he wrote, was expressing "the pure milk of the master-race doctrine" and presenting it with

> the usual glum sanctimoniousness as a traditional Christian doctrine with no sign that it has ever been questioned... It appears that if you have to pinch Caliban black and blue as soon as he stops chopping wood, that is rather like keeping a vow

"holy magic". Was he right?

Renaissance Neo-Platonism underpinned most bookish and scholarly magic (as opposed to the dirty old woman at the bottom of the village dabbling herbs and spells). One of the chief sources for esoteric knowledge and magic was the Hermetic tradition. This derived from a mythological figure called Hermes Trismegistus, an Egyptian writer who pre-dates Plato and Moses and whose ancient religion was supposed to provide the unified source of both pagan and Christian truth.

Hermetic tradition equated the ancient religion and civilisation of its founder with the Golden Age when virtue, love and peace reigned. (There are various references to the Golden Age in *The Tempest*: Gonzalo talks about it the most – in an early speech where he also talks of the idea of a regained Paradise.)

Magic was a serious part of Hermetic philosophy and there were two kinds: goetic – or "black" – magic and theurgic – or divine – magic. Theurgic magic relied upon the soul rising up through contemplation to achieve

of chastity. I must say I wouldn't like to run into a Moral Critic [like Traversi] on a dark night: there is something very shambling and subhuman about the whole movement.

But although Empson has no sympathy with the Prospero who "makes Caliban scream all night", he also argues that it is historically, as well as critically, wrong to suppose that Prospero was "designed to symbolise the White Man's Burden, or to support what Macaulay called the 'nigger-driving interests'". That, he suggests, "does a moral injustice to Shakespeare and his audiences".

---

unity with God, and was more the province of learned scholars and well-educated princes than filthy old hags like Sycorax.

On one level, the division between the magic of Sycorax and Prospero's magic is perfectly clear. One is goetic, the other theurgic. Frank Kermode says firmly that Sycorax

> is a practitioner of 'natural' magic, a goetist who exploited the natural sympathies, but whose power is limited by the fact that she could command, as a rule, only devils and the lowest order

of spirits. Prospero, on the other hand, is a theurgist, whose Art is to achieve supremacy of the elementary, celestial and intellectual worlds... ascending through the created worlds to the condition of angels... His art is "the absolute perfection of Natural Philosophy" [the quote is from Cornelius Agrippa]. Natural Philosophy includes the arts of astrology, alchemy, and ceremonial magic, to all of which Prospero alludes... The point here is that his art, being the art of supernatural virtue which

In this respect, Empson's essay was a warning against future attempts to read *The Tempest* as a colonialist text or play about the New World. The warning went unheeded. Since the 1980s, the American new historicists and the British cultural materialists have read the play from Caliban's, rather than Prospero's, point of view. Such readings have been very influential, are perhaps still dominant, and are always strongly "anti-Prospero". Stephen Greenblatt, for example, says "it is very difficult to argue that the play is *not* about imperialism" and writes with great passion about the "inconsolable human pain and bitterness"

belongs to the redeemed world of civility and learning, is the antithesis of the black magic of Sycorax.

Kermode overstates the case here, and critics like Stephen Orgel and Margreta da Grazia have argued that in fact there is not a lot to distinguish between Prospero's "holy" magic and Sycorax's "devilish" magic. Prospero's art is ambiguous, to say the least. In the play we feel it is dangerous and not entirely civilised.

And is it really holy? Those who argue that it can be squared with Christianity hit one great difficulty: in his great farewell to his "art" or magic, Prospero says quite explicitly that he has raised the dead from their graves, which is unthinkably wicked in Christian terms, or, as Sir Peter Hall has put it, "blasphemous".

Moreover, his famous speech insisting that life itself is an illusion is at least questionable or eccentric in Christian (though not in Buddhist or Hindu) terms.

There is yet another peculiar difficulty in squaring Prospero's magic with Christian teaching. If we regard *The Tempest*

of oppressed, dispossessed natives in the New World – even though, as the critic E.E. Stoll observed in 1927, there is not a *word* in *The Tempest* about America or Virginia, colonies or colonising, Indians or tomahawks, maize, mocking birds or tobacco.

Moreover, in their anti-colonialist and anti-imperialist zeal, these American critics sometimes seem eager to arraign the British past, as though imperialism was strictly a British and European affair, while ignoring their complicity in the more recent history of American imperialism. (See p 44)

Harold Bloom, Greenblatt's great rival as

---

as a play about a magus or magician, its great predecessor (or rival) was Marlowe's *Doctor Faustus*. Faust sells his soul to the devil in return for knowledge, and the agent who then carries out his commands is Mephistopheles, who clearly comes from hell – another world. But the extraordinary thing about Shakespeare's Ariel is that he/she is a "spirit" who doesn't come from another heavenly or hellish world, like Mephistopheles.

Like Prospero's magic, Ariel too has an edge of ambiguity: in part at least

he/she is a fairy and fairies were pre-Christian pagan, and not at all angelic. Ariel is quite unlike the "affable Archangel" Raphael who helps Adam and Eve in *Paradise Lost*.

Ariel - and especially his songs – is evidently part of this world, or our world. If anything, Shakespeare suggests that there is another world, but that it is inside this one.

Christianity sometimes enters Shakespeare's tragedies, but always as a source of further terror, never of consolation. It never enters *The Tempest*,

Emperor of American Shakespeare Studies, is nearly apoplectic about the way in which Caliban, "though he speaks only a hundred lines in *The Tempest*, has now taken over the play":

Caliban, a poignant but cowardly (and murderous) half-human creature... has become an African-American Freedom Fighter. This is not even a weak misreading: anyone who arrives at that view is simply not interested in reading the play at all. Marxists, multiculturalists, feminists, nouveau historicists – the usual suspects – know their causes but not Shakespeare's plays.

although the play recalls several passages from the Bible, which Shakespeare knew very well. Prospero uses his magic – or Ariel – to summon classical goddesses like Iris, Ceres and Juno (though not Venus), but there is no sense of their being "real" deities who have come from Olympus. The goddesses are impersonated by Ariel and his company of spirits, who are otherwise invisible but paradoxically "real" – part of this world.

There were atheists in the Renaissance, just as there are atheists in Shakespeare's plays – not just villains like Edmund or Iago, but casual atheists like Claudio in *Measure for Measure*. Since atheism was punished very severely, however, anti-atheistic tracts were being published long before books that declared and recommended atheism began to appear in the 18th century. A further difficulty was that Renaissance science presented no alternative theory of creation. The dramatist Marlowe was suspected of atheism; Shakespeare may or may not have been or become a non-believer, we simply do

Although Bloom, like Empson, is no admirer of Prospero, he protests that the most recent "anti-Prospero" readings come from critics with a political or cultural axe to grind, not new insights into the text.

None of this, of course, contradicts the fact that Prospero's behaviour in the play – his rages, his cruelty and his urge to control others – makes it hard to sympathise with him, and Bloom's own reading of the play is by no means a "pro-Prospero" one. Prospero's defects may have been exaggerated by partisan critics, but this doesn't make them any the less real. It's important to stress, however, that if we think there's something wrong with Prospero, it does not follow that there is something wrong

not know. But so far as *The Tempest* is concerned, the play's intense reticence or silence about what might be called "official" religion has to be set against the way in which it vibrates with a sense of mystery that many people have thought religious. But the mystery in *The Tempest* can be seen as this-worldly, not other-worldly.

In creating this sense of mystery Shakespeare leaves much unexplained: we are never shown how Prospero does his magic, for example, in the way that, say, Milton delights in telling us how angels can make love without physical friction, changing their gender whenever they please. *The Tempest* is a fantasy, but a dark, sceptical fantasy – more Philip Pullman than Milton or C.S. Lewis – and entirely consistent with the spirit of Hamlet's famous remark: "There are more things in heaven and earth, Horatio, than are dreamt of in your philosophy." ◆

with the play (or Shakespeare). As the great Kenyan writer Ngugi Wa Thiong'o observed in *A Grain of Wheat*, Shakespeare's presentation of the relationship between Prospero and Caliban dramatised but did not cause "the practice and psychology of colonisation".

As for Caliban – he knows he must remain a slave for as long as Prospero is alive or living on the island. He hates being enslaved, hates being kept in a cave instead of having the freedom to roam the island he regards as "mine", and hates being tortured whenever he complains – even "for a trifle", as he puts it.

It is only natural that his dreams of freedom should slide into dreams of killing Prospero – "paunching him with a stake", or "slitting his throat" – just as he dreams of raping Miranda, the only woman on the island. Just as clearly, Prospero cannot allow Caliban to kill him or rape Miranda. But the play certainly *doesn't* suggest that enslaving and torturing Caliban is the solution.

Isn't Prospero right when he describes Caliban as "a born devil"?

It's easy to demonise Prospero, but it's equally easy to sentimentalise Caliban. As Stephen Greenblatt points out, "Caliban is anything but a Noble Savage": he is "deformed, lecherous, evil-smelling, idle, treacherous, naïve, drunken, rebellious, violent, and devil-worshipping". And yet, although Caliban is a savage, his behaviour is no more savage than that of the master who punishes him so horribly, and far less savage than that of the "civilized" but treacherous, murderous Antonio and Sebastian – whom Prospero himself describes as "worse than devils".

Again we might remember how this play began by questioning the categories and distinctions that we use so confidently: "What care these roarers for the name of king?" *Macbeth* was profoundly concerned with what it is, or is not, to be "manly", and in his first historical plays Shakespeare's interest in Queen Margaret and Joan of Arc showed him thinking about what being "womanly" includes or excludes.

In the same way, *The Tempest* is profoundly concerned with what it means to be "human". We constantly prevaricate when using such words. When human animals and their priests or witchdoctors devise ingeniously cruel ways of torturing each other – flaying, impalement, and the rest – this immediately distinguishes "human" animals from all the other animals which never torture members of their own species. But instead of seeing this as a distinguishing feature of what it means to be human, we tut-tut about being "inhuman". One reason why Prospero is not more concerned by the tortures he inflicts on Caliban is that he refuses to regard Caliban as human. But this is the psychology of the torture chamber, and it is hard to be sure what should count as cause or effect.

Prospero insists Caliban is not human, but a "born devil". He tells Caliban that he was

got by the devil himself
Upon thy wicked dam [1.2]

Caliban cannot know whether that is true, but how could Prospero himself know who or what fathered the 12-year-old orphan or *enfant sauvage* already on the island when he arrived? Editors sometimes tell us that Ariel must have been Prospero's informant. But could Ariel know that? Sycorax was already pregnant when she was banished from Algeria and shipwrecked on the island.

According to the conventions of poetic drama, a servant or slave would normally speak in "low" prose while a king would speak in verse. But, although Shakespeare uses and even thinks from such conventions, he repeatedly subverts or extends them. In *The Tempest* Caliban frequently speaks in verse, and indeed Shakespeare gives him much of the play's greatest poetry.

To put that in context, as part of this play's constant questioning of categories and conventions, consider the two conspiracies that are hatched in Act Two. The first of these is "high" or serious, involving VIPs who speak in verse throughout. The second is "low" and comic, and involves Caliban and the two sailors, Trinculo and Stephano. But the play stands this "high"/"low" contrast on its head. The lords in question are civilised savages who are much worse – lower in human terms, though not in social terms – than Caliban. Antonio and Sebastian are both vicious bundles of appetite, driven by nothing more than their nickel-nosed, human-predatorial will to power – whereas the powerless Caliban has a very different motive for wanting to kill the "tyrant" who has dispossessed him, enslaved him, and regularly tortures him.

The old poetic-dramatic convention that lords speak "high" verse while those without social rank – sailors, artisans, plebs – speak "low" prose, is being used and subverted. Trinculo and Stephano always speak in low prose, and so does Caliban when he is with them. But the scene presenting the "low" conspiracy begins with the long and powerful verse soliloquy in which Caliban describes the truly terrible

Opposite: The Wreck from The Tempest, Edmund Dulac, 1908

sufferings he has to endure whenever he is slow, or complains. The "tyrant" Prospero then sends in Ariel and the other spirits to torture him into submission:

> *For every trifle are they set upon me,*
> *Sometimes like apes, that mow and chatter at me,*
> *And after bite me: then like hedgehogs, which*
> *Lie tumbling in my barefoot way, and mount*
> *Their pricks at my footfall: sometime am I*
> *All wound with adders, who with cloven tongues*
> *Do hiss me into madness. [2.2]*

The context for this subversion of poetic-dramatic convention is given a philosophical dimension when the old counsellor Gonzalo speculates about

---

PLAYING POLITICS WITH *THE TEMPEST*

When Terry Eagleton called for a "Caliban school of criticism" in 1986, he meant that pro-Caliban readings of this play were needed to challenge and displace all of the past and present pro-Prospero readings. In critical terms, however, pro-Caliban readings inevitably boil down to anti-Prospero readings, since Caliban is a powerless and dispossessed victim while Prospero has all the weapons. In any case, the pro- and anti-Prospero debate had been going for years before Eagleton's intervention, as he must have known.

But what is at issue here is not always, or even primarily, Shakespeare's play. Many of the recent anti-Prospero, anti-imperialist readings boil

the nature of the "islanders" and natives:

> *though they are of monstrous shape, yet note*
> *Their manners are more gentle, kind, than of*
> *Our human generation you shall find*
> *Many, nay almost any. [3.3]*

A few travellers and readers of their tales – most notably the philosopher Montaigne, in his essay "Of the Cannibals" – were similarly disposed to admire some noble qualities in the natives of the New World, as well as their admirable physiques. Although the primitivist idea of the "noble savage" was not yet current, Montaigne argues that so-called savages were frequently better than civilised

---

down to readings that are also, rather transparently, anti-British. The anti-Prospero reading of *The Tempest* has been popular in America precisely because it is anti-British, and as America grew more powerful, and departments of American Literature spread across the world, so the anti-Prospero, anti-British way of seeing the play became more widespread.

The Tempest is not the only literary work to suffer from anti-British feeling.

Joseph Conrad's *Heart of Darkness* was for many years the most frequently taught text in American universities, part of its appeal being that it attacked the then dominant British and European forms of imperialism. For example, the American critic, Thomas Cartelli – who describes Prospero as "a formative producer and purveyor of a paternalistic ideology that is basic to the aims of Western imperialism" – sees

savages – like Antonio and Sebastian.

Shakespeare is clearly drawing on this enthralling essay – written in the 1580s – when, a little later, Gonzalo delivers his utopian fantasy about a commonwealth without any need for laws. The relentless, rancidly cynical interruptions of Antonio and Sebastian show how, on the contrary, laws are necessary to control creatures like them. Once again, this backs up Montaigne's argument

Conrad's deranged, murderous Kurtz in *Heart of Darkness* as "a latent, potential or actualized version of Prospero".

But soon after Conrad had finished *Heart of Darkness* in February 1899 there were two marked waves of furiously anti-American feeling in his correspondence, when it became clear – first, in the so-called Spanish-American wars, and later in the very shady, treaty-breaking American support for a Panamanian Republic that would allow the Panama Canal to be built – that the Republican governments of McKinley and Teddy Roosevelt were themselves pursuing imperialist policies. Conrad's *Nostromo* was the politically prescient result.

Yet American critics from Edward Said down have continued to argue that *Heart of Darkness* was Conrad's greatest achievement, not, as Conrad himself and many British critics supposed, *Nostromo*. For so-called cultural materialists like Eagleton, criticism is "primarily" or "ultimately" political, and this appears to be true when we consider and compare the critical fortunes of *The Tempest* and *Nostromo* in the United States, where so many readers and voters appear to suppose that imperialism was a largely British and European affair that is now safely in the past.◆

that so-called "savages" like the Brazilian Indians, are frequently superior, in human and moral terms, to civilised savages like Antonio and Sebastian. And the play hardly admits any doubt on this matter: Antonio just *is* far worse than Caliban.

To make this dramatic point, Shakespeare makes Antonio so unrelievedly evil that Antonio is interesting only within the "Montaignean contrast", not as a character. In commenting on Antonio and Sebastian's relentless or obsessive sneers at Gonzalo, A.D. Nuttall shrewdly observed:

> Let us not deceive ourselves. Antonio and Sebastian are truly witty; Gonzalo really does talk like an old fool. But Antonio and Sebastian are themselves both foolish and wicked, while Gonzalo is not really a fool at all.

Another way of making that point would be to observe that Gonzalo is given his own voice – that of a basically kindly but prevaricating man who obeyed the command to send Prospero and Miranda off to what appeared to be certain death, but at least provided Prospero with supplies and his most treasured books. In comparison, Antonio's voice is barely distinguishable from Sebastian's. Compared with the scene in which Lady Macbeth persuades Macbeth to kill his king and kinsman, the dialogue in which Antonio persuades Sebastian to kill King Alonso is like a water-colour sketch –

not because Shakespeare is "weary" in *The Tempest* (as Lytton Strachey suggested in a famous or notorious essay), but because Shakespeare's primary interest is to exhibit Antonio and Sebastian as bestial examples of *Old* World savagery.

On the other hand Caliban is given an entirely unforgettable voice. In Shakespeare's time as in our own, Caliban's quasi-legal claim that "This island's mine by Sycorax my mother" is legally dubious, and might be stronger if he did not mention his mother at all. As David Lindley points out in his admirable introduction to the Arden edition of *The Tempest*, he is not an indigenous native, but "rather a first-generation colonist himself. His enslavement by Prospero repeats his mother's earlier imprisonment of Ariel, who might be considered the island's 'real' indigenous inhabitant."* Critics who see Caliban as a victim of colonialism need to take this into account. Nietzsche's famous advice often holds good in this play: we should always doubt whatever we most *want* to believe.

But the extraordinary, densely packed physicality of Caliban's poetry carries a different kind of claim, by showing how he knows and loves every "fertile inch" of his island: its mixture of pleasures and austerities are vividly evoked – the "fresh springs", the "brine pits" and "barren

---

* Ariel initially served Sycorax after her arrival on the island, but eventually disobeyed her and was imprisoned in a tree for doing so, where he remained until set free by Prospero.

places", "the pig-nuts" and "jay's nest", the "nimble marmosets", the "clustering filberts": all of these physical and tactile evocations come from Caliban.

Neither Prospero or Miranda ever speaks of the island like this, or with any kind of appreciation. Prospero tells Alonso that as soon as he arrived on it he determined to "make himself lord on't". But he is no Robinson Crusoe. Even after living on the island for 12 years, he still depends upon Caliban's help in ways that anticipate Hegel's and later accounts of the interdependent relations of master and slave. Prospero never really knows, let alone loves, the island that he leaves as soon as he can, without taking swag but also without regret.

How does Miranda rebel against her father?

Caliban's attempt to rebel against Prospero fails dismally, as it was always sure to, but in Act Three Prospero faces another, more momentous rebellion – which does not fail. It is from his daughter, Miranda, and it can be seen as one of the turning points of the play. Instead of being enraged when his daughter disobeys his commands, Prospero is delighted, and suddenly, in this scene, we are more inclined to feel sympathetic towards him. From the first, Miranda's "pity" and capacity for compassion are emphasised:

O, I have suffered
With those that I saw suffer! [1.2]

In this respect – as feminist critics have often complained – she might seem to be a weaker heroine than, say, Rosalind in *As You Like It*.

Her loving obedience makes her more like Ophelia, so that we might not readily think of setting her values against those of her father. But that possibility is already present in her very first speech, when she says – with a flash of fire and passion:

Poor souls, they perished.
Had I been any god of power, I would
Have sunk the sea within the earth, or ere
It should the good ship so have swallowed, and
The fraughting souls within her.

The powerless Miranda wants her father to be compassionate and not some "god of power" – just as Ariel will later urge Prospero to be "tender".

Many Shakespeare plays, most notably *King Lear* and *Antony and Cleopatra*, oppose love values to power values. Cleopatra regards Octavius Caesar – the divine "Augustus" who is celebrated in so much Roman and English "Augustan" literature – as a barely sexed "boy". But the cold, power-mad "boy" triumphs. In Shakespeare, as in life, the

Opposite: Rachel Kempson (mother of Vanessa Redgrave)
as Ariel at the Shakespeare Memorial Theatre, 1934

contest between power values and love values is usually uneven: the good die unhappily while the bad sleep well.

By the third act Miranda has fallen in love with Ferdinand. Like Caliban in the previous scene, she longs for nothing more than the freedom of serving her own new master – the man she now loves, after all her years as a lovingly obedient daughter. This longing first leads her to disobey her father, and finally leads to what can only be described as a wholly deliberate rebellion against her father's wishes, power and authority.

MIRANDA'S MARRIAGE

In English law at this time, the so-called de praesenti contract, or "handfasting", was legally binding. The "bed tricks" in *Measure for Measure* and *All's Well That Ends Well* depend upon this law. So, in *Measure for Measure*, Angelo is legally betrothed to Mariana but is not legally married to her since their union has not been sexually consummated when Mariana loses her fortune and Angelo abandons her. The Duke then engineers that Angelo will sleep with Mariana while believing that she is Isabella.

The Church strongly disapproved of such unions, but had to compromise by demanding only that such unions be followed by a public ceremony. As a matter of hard economic necessity, it was important for many men to establish that their women were fertile. In recognising the legality of such unions, the law was not encouraging pre-marital sex, but was protecting the mother-to-be and the child.

After telling Ferdinand,

The scene begins with a soliloquy in which Ferdinand complains – like Caliban in the soliloquy that launched the previous scene – that Miranda's "crabbed" father is "composed of harshness". Prospero has insisted that if Ferdinand wants to avoid some more terrible punishment he

> *must remove*
> *Some thousands of these logs, and pile them up [3.1]*

Prospero and Miranda can't need that many fires on their Mediterranean island, but perhaps the

"I am your wife, if you will marry me", Miranda asks him whether he will be her "husband". He replies,

> Aye, and with a heart as willing
> As bondage e'er of freedom.
> Here's my hand. [3.1]

Miranda then gives him hers – "And mine, with my heart in't" – and from this moment they are legally betrothed. They are taking each other as husband and wife, using the present tense (per verba de praesenti) and giving each other their hands, and they will be legally married as soon as this union is consummated.

Many parents disapproved of – or had nightmares about – such unions, because parental consent was not required, so long as the couple were of legal age (14) to enter into such a contract. There is nothing, in legal terms, that Prospero can do to cancel such a union, since Miranda is 14, like Juliet.

In dramatic terms it is also very important that Miranda takes the initiative. In Shakespeare's comedies, as in Erasmus's remarkable colloquies about marriage, the women are usually sexually frank, more honest, and smarter than the men. ◆

pointlessness of lugging thousands of logs from one place to another is the point, like forcing army conscripts to clean latrines with a toothbrush.

Although he has no choice, Ferdinand obeys Prospero's commands willingly, because he thinks serving the "crabbed" father will win him "The mistress which I serve", who already "weeps when she sees me work". Evidently, Miranda has already visited Ferdinand, defying her father. Ophelia betrays the man she loves by obeying her father and brother instead, but when Miranda returns in this scene she disobeys her father, asks Ferdinand to marry her, and swears to be his slave if he will not take her as his wife.

We see another flash of Miranda's passionate nature as soon as she returns, and exclaims:

I would the lightning had
Burnt up those logs that you are enjoined to pile!

She then assures Ferdinand that her father is "hard at study", and "safe for these three hours". Her father is actually watching both of them, where they cannot see him – "above", according to the stage direction – and Prospero comments in an aside:

Poor worm, thou art infected;
This visitation shows it.

He then hears Miranda "pray" Ferdinand to let her "bear your logs" for a while. Then, when Ferdinand asks her name she tells it, while feeling a pang of guilt at this disobedience:

> *O my father,*
> *I have broke your hest to say so.*

She next confesses that she

> *would not now wish*
> *Any companion in the world but you*

and adds guiltily, in a way that doubtless increases her adoring lover's pleasure:

> *I prattle*
> *Something too wildly, and my father's precepts*
> *I therein do forget.*

Ted Hughes described Ferdinand and Miranda as "proper little Puritan puppets". That hardly seems true to the way in which this scene shows Miranda discovering and bravely, even recklessly, following her own passionate feelings. It is hard to feel the same sympathy with Ferdinand, who is a far less interesting character than his predecessor Florizel in *The Winter's Tale*, and had presented Miranda with his princely shopping list as soon as he met her:

> *My prime request,*
> *Which I do last pronounce, is—O you wonder—*
> *If you be maid, or no?* *[1.2]*

The grace and wit of Miranda's reply had then shown how she is more intelligent than Ferdinand, as Juliet is more intelligent than Romeo:

> *No wonder, sir,*
> *But certainly a maid.*

Presumably her father had given her some sex education, although one doesn't like to imagine what he would have said. But in this later scene, Ferdinand is at least intelligent enough to take his lead, like Romeo, from the 14-year-old woman he loves.

At first Ferdinand prattles in his own courtly way, explaining that

> *for your sake*
> *Am I this patient log-man* *[3.1]*

– whereupon Miranda suddenly asks him, in the frank and direct way that is so characteristic of Shakespeare's comic heroines, "Do you love me?" In his more frothing, courtly fashion Ferdinand insists that he does – "O heaven, O earth, bear witness to this sound", etc. – and Miranda weeps "at what I'm glad of". Instead of flying into one of his rages, the concealed Prospero comments, in a delighted and delightful aside:

> *Fair encounter*
> *Of two most rare affections. Heavens rain grace*
> *On that which breeds between 'em.*

This scene then comes to its extraordinary climax when the passionate, rebellious Miranda finally throws all caution to the winds and tells Ferdinand,

> *I am your wife, if you will marry me;*
> *If not, I'll die your maid. To be your fellow*
> *You may deny me, but I'll be your servant*
> *Whether you will or no.*

This moves Ferdinand to kneel to her, and to speak, at last, in a similarly naked, heartfelt and suitably humbled fashion:

> *My mistress, dearest,*
> *And I thus humble ever.*

Miranda presses on, in her passionately plain way: "My husband then?" "Ay," replies Ferdinand:

> *with a heart as willing*
> *As bondage e'er of freedom: here's my hand.*

She gives her own – "And mine, with my heart in't"

– and they are then *married*! (See p. 52)

Prospero himself can do nothing to annul this legal union, and his daughter's sudden and complete rebellion against his own authority. But he does not want to. In the aside that concludes this wonderfully happy scene he says, with a wry but no less wonderful and unexpected humanity:

So glad of this as they I cannot be,
Who are surprised with all; but my rejoicing
At nothing can be more.

When does Prospero decide to be merciful?

In considering how and when Prospero changes, two scenes are crucial. We have just considered the first, when Prospero's response to Miranda is so benevolent. To the producer and director Nancy Meckler, "Miranda is the catalyst of the story. Had it been possible for her to have remained forever a child in a child's body *The Tempest* would have been unnecessary", and the play turns on the power "that parents necessarily have over their children which must be relinquished".

Prospero's delight with what happens in this scene might, as Meckler suggests, signal some change of heart. And Prospero is in a similarly benign mood at the beginning of Act Four, when he tells Ferdinand that he has "stood the test" and can "take my daughter". He also addresses Ariel in a touchingly affectionate way, as "my delicate Ariel", and eagerly instructs Ariel on the "vanity of mine art" that Ariel and his fellow spirits are to present as a masque-like entertainment to celebrate the lovers' forthcoming wedding.

However, Prospero is less benign, and indeed ferocious, in warning the lovers not to consummate their union before the marriage, and suddenly becomes enraged, halting the masque, when he remembers Caliban's "foul conspiracy".* The frightened Miranda says she has never before seen her father "touched with anger so distempered".

Act Four finishes with Prospero telling Ariel what ingenious new tortures to inflict on Caliban:

Go, charge my goblins that they grind their joints With dry convulsions [4.1]

– and so on, for there is more. If, as Nancy Meckler suggests, Miranda was a "catalyst" in the story of Prospero's transformation, that transformation is clearly not yet complete.

But then, just minutes later, we arrive at the most beautiful and astonishing moment in the

*Many directors must have wished the masque stopped much earlier: despite its rich, Keatsian poetry, it is dramatically static and a nightmare to stage, and Harold Bloom describes it, almost venomously, as the play's "nadir".

play, when Ariel, the non-human "spirit", shows that he can be "tender". (He or perhaps she: in her 1996 production for the Shared Experience Theatre Company, Meckler cast the actress Rachel Sanders as Ariel and presented Prospero's relationship with the spirit as analogous to that with his daughter: Sanders's Ariel was, according to one reviewer, "a recalcitrant and other-worldly teenager bowed by parental expectations".)

At the start of Act Five, Ariel assures Prospero that he has carried out all of his instructions, and that Prospero's enemies are now all helpless and "Brimful of sorrow and dismay". But then Ariel tells Prospero that

> *if you now beheld them, your affections*
> *Would become tender.   [5.1]*

"Dost thou think so, spirit?" asks Prospero. Ariel replies, "Mine would, sir, were I human." "And mine shall," says Prospero.

Ariel's reply can be understood – and delivered – in different ways, one of which is not that usually suggested by critics and editors and could be paraphrased as follows: "You, sir, appear to suppose that spirits cannot be 'tender'. But I assure you that I would be 'tender' to these suffering creatures, even if I were human. The question is what will you do, since you are human."

Opposite: Rachel Sanders as Ariel, Shared Experience Theatre Company, 1996

That possibility is also being picked up in Prospero's reply, when he tells Ariel that his own "affections" or feelings are no less "kindlier moved":

> *And mine shall.*
> *Hast thou (which art but air) a touch, a feeling*
> *Of their afflictions, and shall not myself,*
> *One of their kind, that relish all as sharply*
> *Passion as they, be kindlier mov'd than thou art?*

Prospero now affirms that he will be merciful, so long as those who so deeply wronged him are penitent:

> *Though with their high wrongs I am struck to th'*
> *quick.*
> *Yet with my nobler reason, 'gainst my fury*
> *Do I take part: the rarer action is*
> *In virtue than in vengeance: they being penitent,*
> *The sole drift of my purpose doth extend*
> *Not a frown further.*

At last! But when Prospero says, "And mine shall", he *could* be reassuring Ariel that it was never his "purpose" to be vengeful. In that case his grand, mysterious plan or project just *is*, pretty well from first to last, the play we call *The Tempest* – a triumphant projection of Prospero's will and power, and not a journey of discovery for Prospero himself.

Opposite: John Gielgud prepares to play Prospero at the Old Vic, 1930

TEN FACTS
ABOUT *THE TEMPEST*

1.

Since most of Shakespeare's plays include prose, line counts vary from one edition to another. However, *The Tempest* – with 2,600 lines in the Oxford edition, of which Prospero speaks 673 lines – is one of the shortest of Shakespeare's plays. *Hamlet*, at 3,924 lines, is the longest; *The Comedy of Errors*, 1,770 lines, is the shortest.

2.

The Tempest itself would have earned Shakespeare comparatively little – about £6 was the going rate for a finished script. But by 1610 he was making not less than £200 a year, and possibly as much as £700, most of his earnings coming from his shareholding in the theatre company, The King's Men.

3.

By the time he wrote *The Tempest*, Shakespeare was the owner of several properties in and around Stratford, incuding New Place, the second largest house in the town, which he bought in 1597, and 107 acres of farmland and a cottage in Chapel Lane, which he bought in 1602.

4.

Prospero was John Gielgud's favourite role. He played the part four times: first in 1930, when he wore a turban, later confessing that he intended to look like Dante. Other recent Prosperos include Patrick Stewart, Alec McCowen, Derek Jacobi, David Troughton and Vanessa Redgrave.

5.

One of the most famous experimental productions of *The Tempest* was Peter Brook's at the Round House in 1968, which relied heavily on mime. In Jonathan Miller's 1988 production at the Old Vic in London, Prospero was explicitly portrayed as a coloniser and while white actors were cast as humans (Max von Sydow was Prospero), black actors played the spirits and creatures of the island. Several productions, including one at the RSC in 1982, have attempted to show Caliban and Ariel as opposing elements of Prospero's psyche. In another controversial production in 1993, Simon Russell Beale's Ariel was openly resentful of Alec McCowen's Prospero, and when he was finally granted his freedom he spat in Prospero's face.

6.

BBC Radio has aired more than 300 Shakespeare performances in its history, with *The Tempest* proving the most popular, having been produced 21 times. This, and the unevenness of the 1979 BBC TV film, with Michael Hordern as Prospero, may suggest that the play's appeal to the imagination makes it more suited to radio.

7.

The Tempest has been filmed several times, and has also inspired films like *The Forbidden Planet* in 1956. Among controversial adaptations was Derek Jarman's homoerotic *Tempest* in 1980 and Peter Greenaway's 1992 film *Prospero's Books*.

8.

Tchaikovsky wrote an orchestral work called *The Tempest* ; Sibelius wrote a suite for a 1926 production of the play at the Royal Theatre in Copenhagen. Harps and percussion were used to represent Prospero. *Full Fathom Five* and *The Cloud-Capp'd Towers* were two of three Shakespearian songs set to music by Vaughan Williams. Marianne Faithfull recorded her own distinctive version of *Full Fathom Five* in 1965. The most recent, difficult but richly rewarding operatic version of *The Tempest* is that by the young British composer Thomas Adès. Among several traditional but questionably "established" ideas that Adès exuberantly but thoughtfully challenges is the idea that Prospero must be an old, old man who happens to have a 14-year-old daughter.

9.

Among poets to have written works influenced by *The Tempest* are Shelley (*With a Guitar, To Jane*), Robert Browning (*Caliban upon Setebos*) and W.H. Auden (*The Sea and the Mirror*, which takes the form of a reflection by each of the supporting characters in the play on their experiences), and Ted Hughes in some of his Crow poems. At least three important novels have been thought to show some creative response to Shakespeare's play: Joseph Conrad's *Victory*, John Banville's *Ghosts* and J.M. Coetzee's *Disgrace.* In these three cases the extent and significance of the Shakespearean influence might be disputed, but not in the case of Marina Warner's original, rather neglected novel, *Indigo*.

10.

William Hogarth painted his *A Scene from The Tempest* in 1735; Henry Fuseli, in a painting commissioned for the Boydell Shakespeare Gallery in 1789, modelled his Prospero on Leonardo da Vinci; Millais's *Ferdinand Lured by Ariel* (1849-50) is the most important Pre-Raphaelite painting based on the play.

Harold Bloom is one of many critics who suppose that Prospero had "decided upon the 'rarer action' of forgiving his enemies even before he plots to get them under his control."

At no point in the long speech that follows do the words make it unquestionably clear whether Prospero had always intended to be merciful, as Bloom maintains, or whether Prospero is changing his mind and deciding to be merciful only in this final scene, when his enemies are so helplessly within his power. In that case the three words "And mine shall" – which, as David Lindley observes, are sometimes "thrown away" in performance – don't

STAGING *THE TEMPEST*

Almost all Shakespeare's plays were first performed at The Globe, which had a large jutting "apron" stage that maximised contact between the actors and the audience. Since the Globe had no roof, performances could only take place while daylight lasted, and had to be cancelled if the weather was bad.

By the time *The Tempest* was ready, however, Shakespeare's company was using Blackfriars – an indoor theatre with artificial lighting. A consort of professional musicians was available, and special effects were possible, so that the new theatre could both satisfy and foster the growing taste for spectacle and music – both so important in *The Tempest* . (Hamlet and many Elizabethans would speak of going to hear a play, but within a few years of the Queen's death Jacobeans

only show Prospero changing his mind. They announce a momentous change of heart, that would then be this play's climax.

These alternative readings of the same speech are mutually exclusive. It is very unfashionable to say so, but they cannot both be right. One is right, the other wrong, but we cannot know which is right. Shakespeare's actors were not burdened with the knowledge that they were performing "our" national classics, and they did not even have a full text of the play – just their own parts and cues. The actor who first played Prospero was the company's great leading actor, Richard Burbage. Over the

had begun to speak of going to see a play.)

King James and his court loved masques – private, lavishly expensive entertainments for which Inigo Jones was constantly devising new effects and tricks. In the Blackfriars, Ariel still couldn't arrive or exit by whizzing across the stage on a wire, because Inigo Jones hadn't yet invented that stage technology. But one curious stage direction for the masque scene in *The Tempest* tells us that the goddess Juno "descends", apparently in her chariot.

That could be managed in the Blackfriars in 1611, but in the Globe she would have had to park her chariot and walk on like the other goddesses.

In Shakespeare's lifetime people went to new plays, not revivals, and actors often didn't have full texts to work from, just their own parts and cues. So sometimes we don't know precisely what the playwright intended.

In the final scene of *Measure for Measure*, for example, Duke Vincentio proposes to Isabella twice, but never receives an answer or any answer that is recorded

years Burbage had been the first Romeo, the first Hamlet, the first Lear, and of course he was close to Shakespeare. Whatever Burbage did at this crucial moment in *The Tempest* would have shown which of the mutually exclusive readings is right. But we do not know what Burbage did with "And mine shall", and the rest of the ambiguous speech.

We can only ask which of the alternative readings makes for a richer, more moving play. I believe the most plausible interpretation is that Prospero's "And mine shall" announces a transformation – a momentous change of heart

in the surviving text of the play. Still, this would have been resolved in non-textual, visual ways in the first performances: either the Duke and Isabella would have exited separately or, more likely, as Shakespeare's comedies usually ended in marriage, they would at last have joined hands and left the stage together. There would be no room for doubt, of course, if Shakespeare had left stage directions as lengthy as those of George Bernard Shaw or as precise as those of Ibsen. But he didn't and didn't need to, because he was supervising the performances himself.

In the final scene of *The Tempest* Prospero says they will "all" leave for Milan, which seems to include Caliban – though obviously not Ariel. (One famous pictorial record of a typical final, unbelievable tableau in a celebrated Victorian production shows Caliban, finally left alone on his island. Another shows Ariel, happily alone and in mid-air.) But does Caliban really long for his freedom, or does he really want to go on serving his "god" Prospero? We can never know for sure. ◆

that Ariel has helped to bring about, but may also have begun when he was delighted, not enraged, by his daughter's passionate rebellion against his authority and power. In her very first words to her father, Miranda had begged him not to be pitiless; in the final scene Ariel is cautiously urging "Sir" to be tender, not vengeful.

Now, in this moment of recognition (or *anagnorisis,* to use the classical term), Prospero himself understands that he has not known what he really wanted, when he was driven by rage and by his bitter sense of the atrocious "high wrongs" that still strike him "to the quick" at the beginning of this final scene. He tells Ariel to "release" the prisoners, and in the long, famous speech that immediately follows – he resolves to surrender his magical powers, break his staff and "drown my book".

Just before he was dragged down to hell, Marlowe's terrified Faust promised: "I'll burn my books". Hell will not gape for Prospero when he drowns his book. But choosing "virtue" not vengeance and "relinquishing" power has its own cost. The triumphant Prospero will return to Milan as a diminished man, whose daughter will go to live in Naples with her husband, and whose every third thought will be of his "grave".

The idea that Prospero changes is consistent with the impression *The Tempest* gives that much of what happens in life is "out of control", as the author and biographer Charles Nicholl has put it. We have "a sense of supernatural agency guiding our footsteps, even though we don't quite know what we're doing at the time". This applies to Prospero as well as to his victims; even he never quite seems quite in command of events.

Smaller interpretative choices must also be made in any production or mental staging. When Prospero forgives the "three men of sin", Antonio and Sebastian are not penitent at all. Is Prospero under the illusion that they are? Or has he realised that even he, with all his magical powers over the world within the world we call the real world, and with Ariel and the other spirits at his disposal, has been able to change little or nothing in the real world?

In a way, however, the very lack of penitence from Antonio and Sebastian makes Prospero's gesture all the more significant. They have done nothing to deserve forgiveness and there is no suggestion that they are either redeemable or in any way redeemed by their experience, but this makes Prospero's forgiveness seem more real. Antonio, the worst of the villains, remains intractable: his unrepentant silence at the end of the play offers no sentimental resolution. Shakespeare is particularly good at endings involving an unrepentant and disturbingly silent villain. Iago in Othello refuses to say why he did what he did, and his last words are:

SIX KEY QUOTES

" You taught me language; and my profit on't
Is, I know how to curse: the red plague rid you,
For learning me your language. " Caliban [1.2]

" Full fathom five thy father lies,
Of his bones are coral made:
Those are pearls that were his eyes,
Nothing of him that doth fade,
But doth suffer a sea change,
Into something rich and strange. " Ariel [1.2]

" How many goodly creatures are there here!
How beauteous mankind is! O brave new world,
That has such people in't! " Miranda [5.1]

"   We are such stuff
As dreams are made on; and our little life
Is rounded with a sleep. " Prospero [4.1]

" A devil, a born devil, on whose nature
Nurture can never stick: on whom my pains
Humanely taken, all, all lost, quite lost. " Prospero [4.1]

" Where the bee sucks, there suck I
In a cowslip's bell I lie;
There I couch when owls do cry.
On the bat's back I do fly
After summer merrily:
Merrily, merrily shall I live now
Under the blossom that hangs on the bough. " Ariel [5.1]

Demand me nothing: what you know, you know
From this time forth I will never speak word.
[5.2]

Prospero releases Ariel, too, and accepts his responsibility for Caliban, whom he also forgives. The scene in which he does this has caused much critical dispute. "These three have robbed me," Prospero says to Alonso, meaning that Trinculo, Stephano and Caliban have stolen clothes that belong to him. He goes on to talk of how Caliban – "this demi-devil" – has plotted with the others to take the King's life:

Two of these fellows you
Must know and own; this thing of darkness, I
Acknowledge mine.   [5.1]

To one critic, Lorie Leininger, it is as if Prospero is taking possession of Caliban, like a slave owner after a public disturbance saying "Those two men are yours; this darkie's mine." And for 20th-century writers like Robert Graves and Ted Hughes, Prospero was a malign and sinister portent. However, the text – and the whole dynamic of the play itself – allow for a softer, less harsh interpretation of what Prospero means when he acknowledges "this thing of darkness".

A few moments later, he tells Caliban to go with his companions "to my cell":

> *as you look*
> *To have my pardon, trim it handsomely.*

Throughout the play, Caliban has never been allowed to enter Prospero's cell, but now he is being told to go there and clean it up and there is even talk of a pardon. Caliban is immensely relieved and grateful:

> *Ay, that I will, and I'll be wise hereafter,*
> *And seek for grace.*

We don't have to follow the Christian critics who swoon when the word "grace" is used in the final scenes of this play or *The Winter's Tale* to see how this scene confirms the change in Prospero. Having planned the tortures that are to be inflicted on Caliban that night, he is now calling off the goblins.

How much weight should we attach to psychological readings of the play?

Prospero's resonant but ambiguous words about Caliban – "This thing of darkness I acknowledge mine" – have been seen as important in various different, psychological readings of this play.

For example, in the entertaining and clever

sci-fi film *Forbidden Planet*, which freely adapts *The Tempest* , Caliban is the Freudian "Id", and a part of Prospero's own nature or psyche that has become violent and destructive because he has suppressed and refused to acknowledge it. Some searching and serious psychological readings – like that of Meredith Ann Skura – similarly suggest that while both Caliban and Ariel are characters in their own right, they also reflect different sides or aspects of Prospero's personality. Ariel, from this perspective, can be seen as representing the imaginative faculty in Prospero, since it is Ariel who "cleaves" to Prospero and comes "with a thought" – whereas Caliban stands for "unregulated passion and rebellious flesh". It is likely, as David Lindley says, that in creating Ariel and Caliban Shakespeare anticipated "such a reading of them", even if he didn't anticipate Freud or his theories.

Skura's reading is Freudian, as is a broadly similar reading by Stephen Orgel, and our responses to both will in part depend on how much credence we give to Freud. His theory of the "Oedipal" complex typifies the difficulty posed by psychological readings, since Freud never explained or tried to imagine what would count as evidence that the theory is untrue.

Several critics, for example, have followed Freud in arguing that Hamlet suffers from the famous complex. He cannot kill Claudius because

Opposite:: film poster for Forbidden Planet, *1956*

Claudius has done what he and all young males secretly long to do – killed Daddy and gone to bed with Mummy. All of Hamlet's references to his father are loving, but that, according to the theory, only shows that he is suppressing the truth. Freud also argued that no woman resists rape with her full strength since, somewhere in her "unconscious", every woman harbours a secret wish to be raped. Well, tell that to Miranda.

In the case of *The Tempest* , Stephen Orgel argues, convincingly, that Prospero sees "his voyage to the island as a way of starting life over again – both his own, and Miranda's". Orgel then goes on to argue that Prospero "has reconceived himself, as Miranda's only parent, but also as the family's favourite child":

> He has been banished by his wicked, usurping, possibly illegitimate younger brother Antonio: the younger brother *is* the usurper in the family, and the kingdom he usurps is the mother. On the island Prospero undoes the usurpation, recreating kingdom and family with himself in sole command.

This, Orgel goes on, "has the shape of a Freudian fantasy". It certainly does, but perhaps not in the sense that Orgel intends.

Meredith Ann Skura goes further in the same direction when she argues that Prospero harbours incestuous feelings for Miranda. Skura presents no specific, textual evidence that Prospero is peculiar and perverted in this way. Rather, she assumes that *every* father has incestuous desires, and that Prospero is no exception. Her corresponding theory that Caliban represents Prospero's "own repressed fantasies" might seem uncomfortably close to the Freudian argument about Hamlet – with the difference that Prospero cannot stop hating and punishing Caliban for attempting to do to Miranda what he secretly longs to do. On the other hand – and there is another hand – many of her arguments and suggestions might make the most seasoned anti-Freudian pause to consider.

For example, her comparison between Prospero's aversion to Caliban and Duke Vincentio's aversion to Lucio in *Measure for Measure** turns, more plausibly, on the idea that Caliban and Lucio are treated cruelly because they both represent the lustful passions that Duke Prospero and Duke Vincentio strive to disown:

> Like Prospero, Vincentio sees his manipulation [of others] as an altruistic means of educating his wayward subjects into chastity, repentance and

*In *Measure for Measure*, the ruler of Vienna, Duke Vincentio hands over the city to his deputy, Angelo, ordering him to deal with the depravity which he, Vincentio, has singularly failed to deal with. But the Duke remains in the background, manipulating the action and finally emerges to settle everything at the end of the play. Although he pardons the foremost sinners, including a murderer, his greatest rage is reserved for the bawdy, down-to-earth Lucio, who insults him and hurts his pride.

merciful mildness; but it seems to serve more private needs of self-definition as well. For it allows him, as "ghostly father", to deny any aggressive or sexual motives of his own, and then allows him to return at the end to claim both power and sexual rewards as he resumes his dukedom and claims Isabella (the heroine of *Measure for Measure*). Vincentio's "Caliban" is the libidinous and loose-tongued Lucio, who not only indulges his own appetites but openly accuses the Duke of indulging his, so that it is unusually clear in this case that the "Caliban" figure is a representation of the Duke's own disowned passions.

So, just as Duke Vincentio becomes irrationally angry with Lucio, and punishes him severely at the same time that he releases the impenitent murderer Barnardine, Prospero becomes enraged with Caliban when he remembers the plot being hatched against him during the performance of the masque. The frightened Miranda says she's never seen him so angry, and the end of Act Four is truly frightening. We see the enraged Prospero joining with Ariel in setting dogs on Caliban, and then devising the horrible tortures that his goblins are to inflict on Caliban – and also, on this occasion, his fellow-conspirators. But then, in the next and final scene, Prospero is resolving to forgive Caliban as he forgives the others, including the utterly impenitent Antonio. This shows far more than a change in his attitude to Caliban, as someone outside himself; rather it testifies to some inner change in his attitude towards the passions he himself has hitherto either indulged or refused to acknowledge.

Skura observes that

> To a man like Prospero, whose life has been spent learning a self-discipline in which he is not yet totally adept, Caliban can seem like a child who must be controlled, and who, like a child, is murderously enraged at being controlled. Prospero treats Caliban as he would treat the willful child in himself.

So, in her account of the end of *The Tempest*, the moment when Prospero acknowledges Caliban as "mine" then shows him moving *for the first time* towards accepting the child in himself "rather than trying to dominate and erase that child in order to establish his adult authority".

In Skura's reading, Prospero experiences the "last resurgence of the infantile self", yearning after the "golden worlds and fountains of youth". What we see, finally, is an old man coming to terms with death and acknowledging the body and what it represents; he has stopped trying to shape the world to his imagination and come to terms with his own "unregulated passion and rebellious flesh". In Skura's view, the story of Prospero concerns "the end of the individual self".

That is certainly one way of thinking about the end of this play, as well as the significance of "This thing of darkness I acknowledge mine." It also reminds us of the wisdom of Freud's idea of the self as a fractious family, in which happiness is unavailable because the wishes of one family member can only be satisfied at the expense of another.

What is distinctive about Shakespeare's use of language in *The Tempest*?

There are still surprisingly few studies of Shakespeare's language and style that explain clearly how his style changed, and why his language is often more difficult than Chaucer's. One exception is Russ McDonald's brilliant essay, "Reading *The Tempest*" (and his book *Shakespeare's Late Style*); another is the younger British critic Simon Palfrey's *Late Shakespeare: A New World of Words*.

Palfrey shows us how the central characters in *The Tempest* each have their own distinctive voice. Caliban, for example, learns his language from Prospero and Miranda, but the way he uses it is very much his own – it is far less abstract than Prospero's. It is more simple in being "noun and task-based", but it is also alive, as Prospero's is not, with an "eagerness of description" that freshens his words as though the words themselves were "still crisp with dew". Caliban, in his mid-twenties, has no prospects. He has been dispossessed and enslaved, and is tortured by the absence of any mate as well as by Prospero. But his world is still, somehow, like that of Miranda in her mid-teens, "a brave new world".

The world the play's older men see and inhabit is different. It or they are driven, like some insane top, by the urge to seize and possess power, and to control others. (It is strange that we have words for all kinds of sickness, but not for the sickness of those who can only feel alive and happy when they are telling others how to live and what to do.)

The world of Ariel, who needs nobody and wants nothing but his freedom, is different again, and in far more radical ways that are not dependent on time or age. When the yellow sands, seas, pearls and more unexpected cowslips appear in Ariel's songs they are also subject to endless transformations, that take place beyond our (phenomenological) constructs of time and space: "Those are pearls that were his eyes." As Simon Palfrey says, Ariel's music "resembles nothing so much as its apparent agent, the sea: Shakespeare's imagination seems at times to chime with Joyce's in *Finnegans Wake*, as sleep, dreams, language and desire find source and model in the cerebral currents of swirling waters."

But while there are clear differences in the way *The Tempest's* characters speak, there are also similarities, and an overall distinctiveness about the play's language which sets it apart from the rest of Shakespeare's canon. In *Reading The Tempest*, Russ McDonald shows us how the words and structure of the play work together and how, just as the play's scenes and situations keep echoing each other, so its language, too, is full of echoes. Take the passage where Miranda expresses her anxiety about the shipwreck.

PROSPERO

Tell your piteous heart
There's no harm done.

MIRANDA

O, woe the day!

PROSPERO

No harm
I have done nothing but in care of thee,
Of thee, my dear one, thee, my daughter, who
Art ignorant of what thou art, naught knowing
Of whence I am: nor that I am more better
Than Prospero, master of a full poor cell.
And thy no greater father. [1.2]

As well as the repeated words and phrases in

this passage, it echoes with what McDonald calls "phonetic duplication": heart/harm; O/woe; my dear/my daughter; naught/daughter; naught/knowing; full/cell; greater/father. And the passage is full of negatives: no, no, nothing, naught, nor, no.

Many of the most famous lines and passages in *The Tempest* depend on such internal echoes for their effect, like Ariel's "Full fathom five thy father lies" and "Where the bee sucks, there suck I", or Prospero's questionable description of Caliban:

A devil, a born devil, on whose nature
Nurture can never stick: on whom my pains
Humanely taken, all, all lost, quite lost. [4.1]

From the first confused call during the shipwreck ("We split, we split, we split") to Prospero's tale of the past ("Twelve year since, Miranda, twelve year since") to what McDonald calls the "pleasing assonantal chiming of the Epilogue", the repetition of words, sounds and phrases is a crucial stylistic device in *The Tempest*, as it is in Shakespeare's last plays generally (see page 91). Along with the rhyming plots, they give the play its peculiar and distinctive flavour; "most listeners find themselves beguiled by the musical repetition of vowels and consonants, reduplication of words, echoing of metrical forms and incantatory effect of the musical design".

The echoing language is evident in Prospero's speeches, when he is ravaged by memories of the past; it is also used very effectively by Antonio when he urges Sebastian to kill his brother.

SEBASTIAN:

> *I have no hope*
> *That he's undrown'd.*

ANTONIO:

> *O, out of that no hope,*
> *What great hope have you? No hope that*
> *way, is*
> *Another way so high a hope, that even*
> *Ambition cannot pierce a wink beyond,*
> *But doubt discovery there. [2.1]*

As well as the repetitions and alliteration in this passage, as McDonald says, we can also catch here "the relentless negatives characteristic of Shakespeare's villains". Antonio is using language almost as a form of hypnosis. Take these lines about Claribel:

> *She that is Queen of Tunis; she that dwells*
> *Ten leagues beyond man's life; she that from*
> *Naples*
> *Can have no note, unless the sun were post –*
> *The man i'th'moon's too slow...*

They don't mean much, but the string of clauses, not a sentence among them, "is calculated to inveigle the auditor into rhythmic sympathy" with the speaker's claims. The diction is extraordinarily simple; in the part quoted no word is longer than two syllables; most are monosyllabic; the phrases "unless the sun were post" and "The man i'the'moon's too slow" are identical in length and regularity and both end with the repeated "o" sound.

Antonio, here, is using verbal tricks to manipulate Sebastian and very effectively, too. It is part of a pattern. If *The Tempest* is a play about the problem of political power, and men's yearning to possess it, it is also, as McDonald shows, a play which questions the power of language itself to construct, impose or distort our sense of what is real. McDonald shows how speakers in *The Tempest* are constantly playing with language, testing it and misusing it, often deliberately.

The whole play, of course, is a trick. The seemingly very real storm at the beginning turns out to be just a trick of Prospero's magic, just as the play itself is a trick of Shakespeare's art. We, the audience, are taken in by a staged illusion. We soon discover that Prospero has deceived us, but we're kept constantly off-balance during *The Tempest*. The action, as McDonald says, is full of instances of misunderstanding, miscommunication and broken-off communication: both the feast laid on for Alonso and his guests and the masque laid on for Ferdinand and Miranda are broken off abruptly, and speeches are often interrupted. We have no idea what to make of some of the sounds, says A.D. Nuttall: "the music in the air, the voice crying in the wave, the 'strange, hollow and confused noise' which accompanies the vanishing of the reapers and nymphs at the end of the masque..." "The isle may be "full of noises", as Caliban says in his most famous speech, but it's not always clear what the noises mean.*

* In his book *The White Goddess*, Robert Graves points out how the confusion of tenses in this speech adds to the feeling it gives us of time being suspended:

Be not afeard. The isle is full of noises,
Sounds, and sweet airs, that give delight and hurt not.
Sometimes a thousand twangling instruments
Will hum about mine ears, and sometimes voices
That if I then had waked after a long sleep
Will make me sleep again; and then in dreaming
The clouds methought would open and show riches
Ready to drop upon me, that when I waked
I cried to dream again.

How seriously should we take Prospero when he argues that life itself is an illusion?

The Tempest is concerned from start to finish – not just in its first scene and Epilogue – with the difficulty of distinguishing between what is real and what is not real. In Act Two, when the victims of the shipwreck take stock of their new situation and location, Lord Adrian (a member of Alonso's court) and the kindly counsellor Gonzalo don't see the same island as the civilised savages, Antonio and Sebastian, illustrating the force of Blake's famous maxim: "As man is, so he sees":

ADRIAN:
    The air breathes upon us here most sweetly.
SEBASTIAN:
    As if it had lungs, and rotten ones.
ANTONIO:
    Or as 'twere perfumed by a fen.
GONZALO:
    Here is everything advantageous to life.
ANTONIO:
    True, save means to live.
SEBASTIAN:
    Of that there's none or little.

GONZALO:

How lush and lusty the grass looks! How
green!

ANTONIO:

The ground indeed is tawny.

SEBASTIAN:

With an eye of green in't.

ANTONIO:

He misses not much.

SEBASTIAN:

No: but he doth mistake the truth totally. [2.1]

In *The Tempest*, as in *Othello*, seeing isn't,
or at least shouldn't be, believing. Everyone is

SHAKESPEARE'S
LATE PLAYS

Critics first began to group
*Pericles, Cymbeline, The
Winter's Tale* and *The
Tempest* together as
"Romances" in the late 19th
century. The new generic
label answered to their
sense, which is not widely
shared today, that these
plays showed Shakespeare
entering a "serene" final
phase of his creative life.

While these terms
have to be treated warily,
especially as regards *The
Tempest*, the last plays do
share certain characteristics
which set them apart: the
first three are all set in
mythical worlds and all four
include elements from
myths and fairy tales. In
the first three plays, the
separation and reunion of
families is a common theme
as is reconciliation, rebirth
and redemption. Another

deceived. Even when the happy couple, Ferdinand and Miranda, are "discovered" playing chess in the final scene, Miranda suggests that Ferdinand has been cheating. Chess was often used as a metaphor for sexual and political intrigue, as in Thomas Middleton's play, *A Game of Chess*, and this seems a bad omen for the future:

MIRANDA:
Sweet lord, you play me false.

FERDINAND:
No, my dearest love,
I would not for the world.

recurring preoccupation is the relationship between "nature" and "nurture".

Frank Kermode put it this way in 1954:

All the romances treat of the recovery of lost royal children, usually princesses of great, indeed semi-divine, virtue and beauty; they all bring important characters near to death, and sometimes feature almost miraculous resurrections; they all end with the healing, after many years of repentance and suffering, of some disastrous breach in the lives and happiness of princes, and this final reconciliation is usually brought about by the agency of beautiful young people; they all contain material of a pastoral character or otherwise celebrate natural beauty and its renewal.

There are other common themes, too. As Russ McDonald points out, illusion and reality – and the limits of our understanding of the world – are very much a part of all four plays. What

MIRANDA:
> *Yes, for a score of kingdoms you should wrangle,*
> *And I would call it fair play.* [5.1]

Nobody else notices or says anything about this. But then, just moments later, we have Miranda's ecstatic hymn to the "brave new world":

> *O wonder!*
> *How many goodly creatures are there here!*
> *How beauteous mankind is! O brave new world*
> *That has such people in't!*

This – said to a collection of dazed sinners and

---

we see depends on where we stand. The romances, says McDonald, "insist on the value of proper perspective, on the dangers of solipsism and hubris, on the inevitable limitations of our understanding". *The Winter's Tale* famously blurs the distinction between the actual and the artistic, he says, "by inviting us to fall in love with various forms of illusion, above all with Hermione's statue and, that which it represents, the play itself".

Several critics, notably McDonald and Simon Palfrey, point out that Shakespeare's attitude to women and femininity is subtly different in the late plays, and much more positive than in the plays written immediately before them. The tragedies preceding the final phase, *King Lear*, *Timon of Athens*, *Macbeth* and *Coriolanus*, are all "fiercely anti-romantic" and present the most negative, "even grotesque" portrayals of female sexuality in the entire canon, says McDonald.

dull courtiers – may merely reflect Miranda's naïveté. No wonder her father simply replies: "'Tis new to thee."

All the illusions of the play get turned on their head at the end in Prospero's "Our revels now are ended" speech when he suggests that what we call "real life" is all an illusion, too – *maya* (illusion) or *mu* (emptiness), in the Buddhist sense:

> *like the baseless fabric of this vision,*
> *The cloud-capped towers, the gorgeous palaces,*
> *The solemn temples, the great globe itself,*
> *Yea, all which it inherit, shall dissolve,*
> *And, like this insubstantial pageant faded,*

Whether or not we think of the women at the end of the romances as returned to the system of male domination, it is clear that Shakespeare's conception and representation of the feminine has changed since he wrote *King Lear* and *Macbeth*.

Simon Palfrey argues that while the stories of the last plays are essentially patriarchal, the way the stories are told is "feminized".

A foolish or venal male hegemony is altered and humanized by the incorporation, as a persuasive instrument of power and decision-making, of a "feminine principle" based not only in the faithfulness of chastity but the eloquence of the female tongue.

In a broader sense, too, the last plays can be seen as more feminine. McDonald quotes Thomas Howell's famous remark in 1581 – "Women are wordes, Men deedes" – and points out that Shakespeare's late style, he thinks – full of wordplay, ambiguity, mystery, artifice and pleasure – is much more feminine than the language of earlier plays.

But all of these arguments – about reconciliation, restoration, femininity and so on – can be pushed too far, as McDonald warns: the last plays are also full of doubt and subversion, and none more so than *The Tempest* .

Derek Traversi, for example, points out that in the last plays there is a close association between supernatural imagery and timeless values like love. In *The Winter's Tale,* Shakespeare compares Perdita to a wave, and this expresses "a vital theme in the play... the relation between the values of human life which postulate timelessness, and the impersonal, 'devouring' action of time which wears these values ceaselessly away".

This may be true, but, as A.D. Nuttall points out, the point is harder to make about *The Tempest*. We are undoubtedly invited to make a connection between the magic practised in the play and the "magic" of Ferdinand and Miranda falling in love – "Love is conceived as a supernatural force", as Nuttall puts it – but the "Affirmation of Paradise" at the end of the play is "far less confident" than it is in *The Winter's Tale, Cymbeline* or *Pericles* (Miranda first sees Ferdinand as if he is something supernatural: "What is't? a spirit?")."In *The Tempest* alone of the romances the divine masque is broken up in confusion. The whole play, as compared with *The Winter's Tale*, is strangely perverse, like a piece of flawed glass... It is as if a second wave of scepticism has passed over the poet."

Shakespeare, in other words, is not denying the authenticity of love in *The Tempest,* but he is expressing reservations as to its value. "After the enthusiastic reaffirmation of the later Sonnets and the first three Romances, a sadder and more complex reaction has set in... The world has not been wholly redeemed by love: look at it. The subjective vision of the lover may transcend objective facts, but it does not obliterate them." ◆

Leave not a rack behind. We are such stuff
As dreams are made on; and our little life
Is rounded with a sleep. [4.1]

This speech has often been compared to Puck's
at the end of *A Midsummer Night's Dream*, but
Puck's speech is more reassuring about what is real
and what is not:

If we shadows have offended,
Think but this, and all is mended,
That you have but slumber'd here,
While these visions did appear... [5.1]

Prospero, on the other hand, is anything but
reassuring. "Puck himself is capable of stepping
outside the play in order to discuss it," says A.D.
Nuttall. In Prospero's speech, "the circle of darkness
continues to widen, passing over the audience itself,
beyond the walls of the theatre, to engulf palace
and church, and, at last, the whole world. From
making the stage shimmer before our eyes Prospero
passes on to cast the same spell of doubt on the
earth itself. Words alone retain a vivid life, cutting
deep at our inmost memories and perceptions."

But even here we must be on guard. This, it
might be said, is just where Prospero *is* at the end
of the play. To say that life itself is an illusion may

Opposite: Ralph Richardson as Prospero in the Royal
Shakespeare Company production in Stratford, 1952

be yet another illustration of Blake's "As a man is, so he sees". If everything is a really an illusion, after all, why should we even be interested by a play that takes such a severe, even cynical view of rulers and the will to power?

During the play, Prospero makes a journey of discovery in which he finally discovers that what he thought he wanted was not what he wanted. The ending of *The Tempest* is both abrupt and unexpected. As in *Measure for Measure* – where Duke Vincentio is Prospero's closest rival as a surrogate dramatist who tries to determine everything that will finally happen – everything that has happened appears to be preparing us for a tragic outcome.

But at the end of *Measure for Measure* Duke Vincentio clings to his fantasy of being godlike, whereas Prospero changes his mind – or heart. *The Tempest* is his story, his psychic journey of self-transformation.

Learning can be dangerous as well as good, and has proved so for Prospero – as it did for Marlowe's Faustus. Prospero became desocialised, lost touch with his court, his kingdom and his subjects, and, perhaps most importantly, with himself. He became passionately bookish, and the "volumes that I prize above my kingdom" were the source of his power. His triumph over himself, and his return to society, are indicated by his renunciation of power – and the drowning of his book. What he himself calls a triumph of "virtue" over "vengeance" is won only after a conquest of himself.

But if, in his final triumph, he is a more sympathetic figure he is also a diminished one. He is old, and about to surrender his daughter as well as his magical powers. As he says in his Epilogue, while he still seems to be speaking in character:

Now my charms are all o'erthrown,
And what strength I have's mine own,
Which is most faint.

What does seem to be clear, by the end of *The Tempest*, is that Prospero's change of heart and his relinquishing of power has a cost. This is another point where the psychological readings – even if they are Freudian, like Skura's, or Lacanian,* like Palfrey's – may have something important to say, to which we should not close our ears. Every father knows the cost of relinquishing power, even when the power he thought he had no longer exists.

* Jacques Lacan (1901-81) was a French psychiatrist and psychoanalyst who was much influenced by Freud but departed from Freud's teachings. His influence has been much stronger in university English departments than in departments of psychology and medicine.

WHAT THE CRITICS SAY

"The Tempest *uncovers, perhaps despite itself, the racist and imperialist bases of English nationalism.*"

[Walter Cohen, 1985]

" *To listen to* [The Tempest's] *language is to become deeply sceptical about the operation of all kinds of power – poetic, political, and critical too.*"

[Russ McDonald, 1991]

"*Is* The Tempest *a Christian play? It is surely a profoundly religious poem, and of a Christ-like spirit in its infinite tenderness, its all-embracing sense of pity, its conclusion of joyful atonement and forgiveness, so general that even Caliban begins to talk of 'grace'. But it is not in the least Christian from the theological standpoint; there is no word of God, not a hint of immortality.*"

[John Dover Wilson, 1950]

"*The most blasphemous play Shakespeare wrote,* The Tempest *is about a man on an island who's allowed to play God and who doesn't just dabble in witchcraft but actually performs it.*"

[Sir Peter Hall, 1988]

"The whole play, as compared with The Winter's Tale, *is strangely perverse, like a piece of flawed glass... It is as if a second wave of scepticism has passed over the poet."*

[A.D. Nuttall, 1967]

"Prospero's Art controls Nature; it requires of the artist virtue and temperance if his experiment is to succeed; and it thus stands for the world of the better natures and its qualities."

[Frank Kermode, 1954]

"The Tempest has two endings: a quiet evening on the island when Prospero forgives his enemies and the story returns to the point of departure; and Prospero's tragic monologue, spoken directly to the audience, a monologue out of time."

[Jan Kott, 1964]

"The Tempest has... been seen as a play about power. Perhaps it should rather be regarded as a play about the illusion of freedom. For if romance offers the chance that time may be redeemed, that utopia may be found, this play's relentless scepticism – about Gonzalo's Golden Age, Ferdinand's paradise and Miranda's brave new world, no less than Caliban's delirious 'freedom, high-day' – seems radically to question its possibility."

[David Lindley, 2002]

So what view of the world does Shakespeare leave us with at the end of *The Tempest*?

Russ McDonald is right that *The Tempest* leaves us feeling sceptical about power in all its forms, not the least of which is the power of art itself. In several passages of *The Tempest* , such as the banquet and masque scenes, Shakespeare underlines the idea that his play is ephemeral and insubstantial. (One way he subtly increases our awareness of his dramatic art is by observing the classical unities, which he does not usually do: in *The Tempest* the action is confined to a single day.)

Just as Prospero and Alonso and their villainous relations try to tame the world and shape it to their will, so artists, in their own fashion, try to do much the same, seeking to reproduce themselves and "to transcend time through art". These efforts represent what McDonald calls "a defence against death" – a kind of subconscious attempt to deny or somehow get the better of death. And they are doomed to failure.

For all its dream-like atmosphere, *The Tempest* is the least sentimental of plays. No play is more insistent about the need to accept uncomfortable realities. Prospero was born a duke but refused to accept the responsibilities that went with his role:

his attempt to escape these responsibilities resulted in his losing power to people most unsuited to wield it, and in his exile and what should have been death. As David Lindley says, his attempt "to find freedom from the active life of office" by retiring to his library delivers him instead to imprisonment on an island where, through finding Ariel and the ability to put his magic into practice, which Ariel facilitates, he gets a second chance – the stuff of dreams.

SHAKESPEARE'S RETIREMENT

It's often been suggested that Shakespeare in *The Tempest* is signalling his retirement. In one of his sonnets (111), he suggests that writing for the public is morally degrading. He complains that he is forced by fortune to earn his living "by public means which public manners breeds"; and he fears that even his inmost nature is becoming stained by vulgarity – almost

> subdued
> To what it works in, like the dyer's hand.

So, perhaps a decade later, Prospero drowns his books and returns to his dukedom; Shakespeare, after making enough money and achieving the rank of "Gentleman" (a real rank, then), happily gave up the stage and retired to the country, to look after his large house in Stratford, his one unmarried daughter and another daughter who was married to an unfaithful husband.

But, again as Lindley says, "the desire through magic to escape from human limitation must itself in the end be disowned". Ultimately magic is not the answer: Prospero has to learn to live with his enemies and to accept his daughter's sexuality; he has to drop his magic and drown his book. For all its emphasis on power, *The Tempest* can also be regarded as a play about the illusion of freedom. For "if romance offers the chance that time may be redeemed, that utopia may be found, this play's relentless scepticism... seems radically to

---

Perhaps, as some have thought, Shakespeare really disliked being a jobbing genius. Others find the idea that Shakespeare was a reluctant dramatist difficult to credit. By the end of the 16th century, his comedies and history plays had already made him the most successful dramatist of his time. He could then have gone on repeating his earlier successes, like many lazy or less than wholly committed artists. Instead, he wrote *Hamlet* and followed through with an extraordinarily, restlessly experimental series of tragedies and troubled comedies. This staggering achievement

came to a climax in the 14 months when he wrote *King Lear, Macbeth* and *Antony and Cleopatra*.

Perhaps, as others have suggested, he then became tired. Later plays followed more slowly; after writing *Timon of Athens* Shakespeare evidently wanted a rest from tragedy. He then began a further series of astonishingly experimental plays. Harold Bloom suggests, darkly, that after the accession of James I Shakespeare became ever more disillusioned with the Court and contemporary London. His imagination was fired when inventing Caliban and Ariel, but

question that possibility".

Shakespeare's comedies usually end with magically charged, exuberant but complex, shadowed conclusions that involve some sense of what must be. But in *The Tempest*, scenes which, in earlier plays, we might have been encouraged to savour are not allowed, in Lindley's phrase, "to resonate fully". Ferdinand and Miranda's reappearance playing chess is threatened by Miranda's "Sweet lord, you play me false" and its characterisation as "A most high miracle" is left to

depressed when it dwelt on contemporary social realities.

Ariel's last, haunting song, "in a cowslip bell I lie" may be relevant here. It has nothing to do with the dramatic situation in the play, but harks back to the fairy world of one of Shakespeare's earliest successes, *A Midsummer Night's Dream*, in which he so exuberantly and lyrically drew upon the country folklore of his childhood in Warwickshire. Ariel's oddly and wonderfully inappropriate song echoes that early play in which scared elves "creep into acorn-cups, and hide them there", and further back to the childhood memories from which his fairy-lore is drawn. Shakespeare was always a country poet, not a city poet like Ben Jonson. Perhaps he became homesick, and longed to return to his roots.

These possibilities are all speculative. Whichever we favour, we should be glad that he was not born a gentleman of leisure and that fortune, or the need to make money, forced him to "degrade" himself by writing for almost the whole of his adult life. Willingly or unwillingly, he became foremost in the first generation of dramatists who made their livings by writing for the public, not for aristocratic patrons.◆

the unpleasant Sebastian, while Alonso's reconciliation with his son is also quickly cut short - by Prospero's "There, sir, stop".

The Tempest is a play that shows us truths in a contained, isolated world which mirrors and exaggerates the "real" world, as in a dream which the play so much resembles. It leaves us with the feeling that life disappoints, that our expectations are rarely, if ever fulfilled, and that for all the beguiling power of words and music and art we must be extremely careful about what we believe. The masque and the banquet are both interrupted. Within hours of meeting Miranda, Ferdinand seems to be deceiving her, her brave new world is briskly undercut by Prospero, as earlier is Gonzalo's utopian speech by the behaviour of Antonio and Sebastian. "Freedom, high-day! high-day freedom!" exults Caliban in Act Two but his real choice, at the end, seems to be continued service to Prospero or a lonely future on the island. Ariel's future, on the other hand, seems likely to be happy, but Ariel is a spirit.

As the play ends, few would dispute Prospero's decision that the rarest virtue is mercy, not vengeance, even though this requires that he must forget his earlier condition that those who wronged him so atrociously must be penitent. In this case the shadow is indeed dark but, like life itself, better than the alternative. Although some

Opposite: Tony Haygarth as Caliban at The National Theatre, 1988

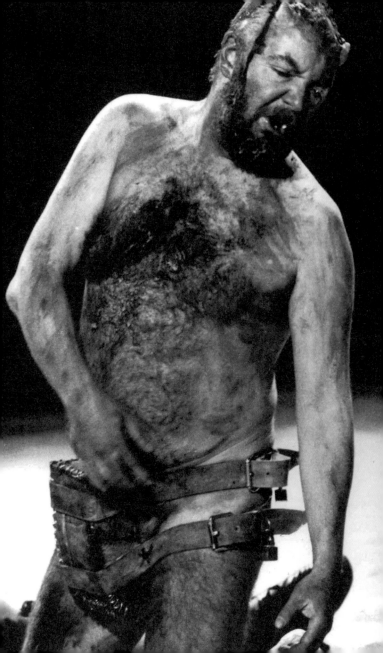

critics suppose that Prospero does not realise that his brother is entirely impenitent, this seems unlikely. It is more plausible that Prospero realises that, even with his magical powers and the services of Ariel and his invisible cohort at his disposal, he can change very little in the word he must now inhabit. So, at the end, he is both triumphant and much diminished – a lonely old man who knows that he has lost his daughter forever, and, for whom, from now on, every third thought will be of "his grave". He has accepted life as it is, and can now hope to be loved, not merely obeyed. *The Tempest* was also, was perhaps primarily, a tempest in him, and it is over. He has finally come to terms with being human.

Theatre programme, 1904

A SHORT CHRONOLOGY

1564 Shakespeare born in Stratford-on-Avon, possibly but not certainly on 23 April. The idea that the Bard must actually have been born on St George's Day is patriotic but historically dubious.

1590-92 *Henry VI parts I, II, and III.*

1596-7 *King John* punctures the doctrine of the divine right of kings in so many ways that it is difficult to suppose that Shakespeare continued to believe in it. Critics have tended to ignore this play.

1599-1600 *Hamlet*. Shakespeare's prince dominates his play to an extent that is rivaled only by Duke Vincentio and Prospero. All three of these characters are also surrogate dramatists who control the action of the plays they inhabit – *Hamlet* in the central acts of his play, Vincentio in the second half of *Measure for Measure*, and Prospero throughout *The Tempest* . This double dominance has encouraged critics to suppose, illogically, that if anything is wrong with these three characters something must be wrong with their plays.

1603 Michel de Montaigne's essay, "Of Cannibals", first translated into English from French by John Florio, though it had been written about 20 years earlier. Florio was a friend of Ben Jonson, who was a friend of Shakespeare, and plays like *Hamlet* and *All's Well That Ends Well* show that Shakespeare was familiar with Florio's Montaigne before it was published.

1604 *The Tragical History of Doctor Faustus* first published, eleven years after Marlowe's death and at least 12 years after its first performance.

1605-06 *Macbeth*

1606 Erasmus's *Naufragium* (*The Shipwreck*), one of many possible sources of *The Tempest,* is translated into English. It was originally published in 1523.

1608 *Pericles,* followed in the next two years by *Cymbeline* and *The Winter's Tale.*

1608-09 John Dee, a celebrated English mathematician, astronomer, astrologer and occultist, dies. Born in 1527, he studied both science and magic and immersed himself in Hermetic philosophy. It has often been suggested that he was the inspiration for Prospero.

1609 The Sea Venture is wrecked on the coast of the Bermudas on her way to Virginia. Amazingly, her passengers, Sir Thomas Gates, Sir George Summers and others, all survived. Shakespeare may or may not have read an account of this before writing *The Tempest* . No one knows. Though not officially published till 1625, William Strachey wrote and circulated his eyewitness report on the real-life shipwreck of the Sea Venture in 1610. Another survivor, Silvester Jourdain, also published an account (*Discovery of the Barmudas*).

1610-1611 Shakespeare writes *The Tempest* . This was not, historically, his last play (or last word on life), since *Henry VIII* and *Two Noble Kinsmen* were written later. How far these plays were collaborations (like the earlier *Pericles*) is still disputed.

1611 1 November. First performance of *The Tempest* by the

King's Men before James I and the royal court at Whitehall Palace. The play was later staged at the Blackfriars Theatre, and probably in the rebuilt Globe Theatre.

1613 The play is chosen to be part of the celebrations in honour of the marriage between James I's daughter, Elizabeth, and the Elector of Palatine.

116 23 April Shakespeare dies.

1623 John Hemming and Henry Condell, fellow-actors and shareholders in the theatre group, the King's Men, publish a collected edition of Shakespeare's works, beginning with *The Tempest*, which becomes known as the First Folio.

1667 William Davenant and John Dryden turn Shakespeare's play into *The Tempest, or the Enchanted Island*. This successful extravaganza, in which Caliban and Miranda both have sisters, Prospero has an adopted son, and Ariel has a sweetheart, held the stage until the actor-manager William Charles Macready restored Shakespeare's text in 1838. An earlier attempt by the great actor David Garrick to restore more of Shakespeare's play had met with little success. Theatregoers without access to the rather expensive reprints of Shakespeare's works could not have been familiar with his very different play. It is sometimes forgotten than when Romantic critics like Coleridge, Keats and Shelley maintained that it was best to read Shakespeare, they were protesting that the texts used for staged performances of plays like *King Lear*, *Macbeth* or *The Tempest* were travesties.

BIBLIOGRAPHY

Empson, William, "Hunt the Symbol" in *Essays on Shakespeare*, Cambridge University Press, 1986

Leininger, Lorie Jerrell, "The Miranda trap: sexism and racism in Shakespeare's *The Tempest*", in *The Woman's Part*, edited by Carolyn Lenz, University of Illinois Press, 1980

Lindley, David, *The Tempest* (ed.), New Cambridge Shakespeare edition, 2002

McDonald, Russ, *Shakespeare's Late Style*, Cambridge University Press, 2006; "Reading *The Tempest*", *Shakespeare Survey 43* (1991), reprinted in *Critical Essays on Shakespeare's The Tempest* (edited by Virginia Mason Vaughan and Alden T Vaghan), GK Hall & Co, 1998

Nuttall, A.D., *Two Concepts of Allegory*, Routledge & Kegan Paul Ltd, 1967

Palfrey, Simon, *Late Shakespeare: A New World of Words*, Oxford University Press, 1997

Skura, Meredith Anne, "Discourse and the Individual: The Case of Colonialism in *The Tempest*", *Shakespeare Quarterly 40:1* (1989), reprinted in Bloom's *Shakespeare Through the Ages: The Tempest*, Infobase Publishing. 2008

Traversi, Derek, *Shakespeare: The Last Phase*, Harcourt, Brace & Company, 1953

[The Globe Theatre, Bankside.]

INDEX

First published in 2012 by
Connell Guides
Spye Arch House
Spye Park
Lacock
Chippenham
Wiltshire SN15 2PR

10 9 8 7 6 5 4 3 2 1

Picture credits:
p 13 ©John Prat / Getty Images
p 21 © CSU Archives / Everett Collection / Rex Features
p 29 © The Globe
p 43 © Christie's Images / CORBIS
p 51 @ Gordon Anthony / Getty Images
p 61 @ Mike Kwasniak
p 63 @ Hulton-Deutsch Collection / CORBIS
p 77 @ SNAP / Rex Features
p 89 @ Bolton Museum and Art Gallery, Lancashire / The Bridgeman Art Library
p 97 @ Everett Collection / Rex Features
p 107 @ National Theatre
p 108 @ Michael Diamond/ ArenaPAL
p 115 @ The Print Collector / Alamy
A CIP catalogue record for this book is available from the British Library.

ISBN 978-1-907776-05-2
Assistant Editor: Katie Sanderson
Design © Nathan Burton

Printed in Great Britain by Butler Tanner and Dennis

www.connellguides.com